SOME OF MY BEST FRIENDS

Essays in Gay History and Biography

A. Nolder Gay

**Union Park Press
Boston
1990**

Union Park Press, P. O. Box 2737, Boston 02208

© 1990 by Union Park Press. All rights reserved.

General Design by: Bruce M. Howden
BMH *graphic design & printing*
32 North Champlain Street
Burlington, Vermont 05401

Cover design: Jim O'Donnell
BMH *graphic design & printing*

Printed in the United States of America.

ISBN 0-9601570-1-8

Original material from Bay Windows (1523 Washington St., Boston, MA 02118; $40.00 per year) © 1983, 1984, 1985, 1986, 1987 by Union Park Press and Bay Windows, Inc.; reprinted by permission of the editor, Jeffery S. Epperly. Original material from *Esplanade*, © 1976, 1977, 1978 by G. W. and M., Inc.; reprinted by permission of the former publisher, Joseph Leo. Original material from *Gay Community News* (62 Berkeley St., Boston, MA 02166: $39.00 per year) © 1974, 1976 by GCN, Inc.; reprinted by permission of the former coordinating editor, Marc Stein; Original material from *Integrity Forum,* © 1979, 1980, 1981, 1982 by Union Park Press and Integrity, Inc.; reprinted by permission of the former editor, Fr. Grant Gallup.

For Jim Saslow,
Scholar, Guide, Friend

Contents

Preface	ix
Part One: Echoes From Antiquity	1
Recovering the Classics (1985)	3
Renault Remembered (1984)	5
Thebes: The Untold Story (1986)	8
Antique Casts (1974)	10
Romans Noble and Ignoble (1977)	12
Un-Mitigated Gaul (1987)	14
Part Two: Continental Sophisticates	17
Learning to Look (1987)	19
Venice Re-Observed (1985)	21
Losing One's Head (1976)	23
An Old Spanish Tale (1986)	26
A Neglected Lesbian Artist (1984)	28
Freudian Odyssey (1984)	30
Procession of Boys (1983)	33
Part Three: "But We Don't Do That; We're British!"	37
A King's Minion (1986)	39
Room at the Top (1976)	41
Bountiful Affections (1977)	43
Beyond the Statistics (1987)	47

Paradise Ungained (1983)	49
The Higher Sodomy and the Biographer's Art (1985)	52
Radclyffe Revisited (1986)	54
Paederistic Evangel (1984)	56
Part Four: All-American Boys	61
Only the Hairdresser Knew (1985)	63
Swishing Through Georgia (1977)	65
Whitman Revisited (1985)	68
All That Glitters (1977)	70
A Gay Academic Scandal (1977)	73
A Forgotten Gay Novelist (1977)	77
Public (and Private) Affairs (1984)	80
Part Five: Sex in the Sacristy	83
Sex and the Single Priest (1981)	85
A Tale of Four Churches (1980)	87
A Memorable Gay Hoax (1980)	91
Gregory's Angels and All That (1981)	94
Bloody Hands, Clean Consciences (1975)	96
Saints Preserve Us! (1987)	99

Part Six: Gay Landscapes 103

    Franciscan Odyssey (1987) 105

    Sicilian Fantasy (1984) 107

    Neapolitan Journey (1985) 110

    Sounding the Sirens (1984) 113

    A Bavarian Fantasy (1986) 115

    Stranger in Paradise (1983) 118

    White Mykonos (1987) 121

Part Seven: Making One's Own Gay History 125

    Celebration (1974) 127

    Out of the Closet and Into the Flicks (1974) 128

    Some Infamous Gay Homophobes (1980) 130

    Playing With Words (1980) 133

    Anita Redux (1981) 136

    Of STD's and Magic Bullets (1986) 140

    Samaritans All (1986) 142

Part Eight: Two Days, a Seemingly Fictional Memoir 145

    Prefatory Note (1989) 147

    Two Days (1980) 148

SOME OF MY BEST FRIENDS

Preface

As I observed in an early column (not here reprinted), "When you arrive at an age when the only guys hot after your bod are morticians, the second best way of curling up in bed is with a good book." The degree of goodness of this book is primarily a function of the memorable gay characters who inhabit it. Because from a very young age I have liked to read, especially to read history and biography, people living in other times and places have always been "some of my best friends." In recent years, "some of my best friends" have been gay.

I began writing essays for gay readers in Boston and elsewhere in 1973. In 1977 I collected and revised a number of early columns, largely reflecting the bemusement of an older gay person "coming out" in Boston in the 1970's. These appeared in 1978 in a volume called *The View From the Closet: Essays on Gay Life and Liberation*. A few of those essays were historical and biographical (and some are reprinted in this collection), but most were written out of my own daily round of experience in and out of the gay movement.

I had written successively for *Gay Community News, Esplanade,* and *Integrity Forum,* until the latter was closed out late in 1982; from time to time, various regional gay papers had reprinted single or several columns. One day early in 1983 I received a call from the editor of a new Boston gay paper, *Bay Windows*. This venture had been begun by Sasha Alyson, publisher and distributor of a growing stock of gay book titles, both fiction and non-fiction.

Bay Windows, it appeared, was looking for someone to write a regular column on gay history. Would I be interested in doing it? I responded that I could not consider one which depended on primary research, like those Martin Duberman had recently been writing for the *New York Native* under the title "About Time." But I could probably churn out the same old A. Nolder Gay-type familiar essays as a byproduct of my reading of other historians and biographers. So they said "fine" and I said "fine" and, with time out now and again for other things, I wrote a monthly column for *Bay Windows* under the general title "Our History" from 1983 until 1987, when the pressure of other writing commitments made it impossible for me to continue it.

These essays are the byproducts of relatively leisured, indeed privileged life-style which has allowed me ample (though never sufficient) time for reading, writing, and travel. Over the last forty years I have travelled intensively over parts of the United States, eastern and western Canada, England, and western and Mediteranean Europe. On my recent European trips I have made it a point to visit places of gay-historical interest, and have kept detailed travel diaries, parts of which have been incorporated in several of the essays in this volume. Other essays reflect serendipitous discoveries made in library stacks or through indulgence in one of my incurable addictions, haunting second-hand bookstores.

Readers will find here no heavy gay liberationist politics; like the patrician early Christian bishop Gregory Julian in the novel *The Sinner of St. Ambrose,* "I would leave parties, dogma, and doctrine to the frantic and insecure: they haven't the heart to live out the day, as themselves, in God's presence, but must busy themselves at browbeating others along paths of alleged perfection." Nor will the reader find much about lesbianism, though I do attempt a couple of lesbian biographies. In spite of my having been made an honorary lesbian at the Integrity national convention in Boston in 1980, I do not have the sensitive nose for the nuances of lesbian history which I think I have for gay male history, so I necessarily leave that line of inquiry to lesbian and women's historians.

Otherwise, there is a potpourri of subjects here: ancient and modern, fact and fantasy, history and geography, the well-known and the obscure. There is perhaps a disproportionate amount of Episcopalian lore, reflecting both my own religious and institutional commitments and the fact that some essays were originally written for an audience of gay Episcopalians and their friends. In the process of revising those essays, I have taken pity on the general reader and cut out some of the more arcane Episcopaliana. But if what remains is bothersome, the reader is free to try something else.

As in my earlier book, I have assigned dates to each of the essays so that they can be fitted into the time-context they reflect. No gay writer of the last six or seven years has written without an ever-present consciousness of the AIDS epidemic, and in several essays I attempted to put this too in some gay-historical frame. Nowadays, more than ever, we in the gay community need to hear and to heed Camus' invitation "to live and to create, in the very midst of the desert." I have found some solace in contemplating the example of Sir Robert Shirley, a 17th century Royalist baronet of Leicestershire, who constructed a chapel in the midst of the chaos following the English civil war. A tablet on the wall of that church describes him as one "whose singular praise it is to have done ye best things in ye worst time, and hoped them in ye most callamitous." It's not a bad model of conduct; one many of us are having to rediscover these days.

In re-releasing these by-products of many satisfying hours as reader, writer, and traveller, I hope that those who have read them before will find pleasure in reading them again, and that those who have not read them in their original form may find here some new and interesting things. For, like Gregory Julian, "I suppose it amounts to this, that some men teach with authority, but the best I can do is stir up wonder and surprise." If a writer is both semi-reclusive and pseudonymous, as I am, securing feedback is difficult. But I do know that at least some of these essays have stirred up wonder and surprise in a few of the gay readers for whom they were originally intended, and that justifies both the effort of writing them and the task of revising them for publication in book form. In this task, I have been greatly aided by my friend Bruce Howden, who has taken responsibility for the overall design and production of the volume. I am also much indebted to Jim O'Donnell, who designed the striking cover.

So, like the writer of Second Maccabees, "At this point I will bring my work to an end. If it is found well written and aptly composed, that is what I myself hoped for; if cheap and mediocre, I could only do my best.... Let this then be my final word."

A. Nolder Gay
November, 1990

Part One:
Echoes From Antiquity

Recovering the Classics (1985)

In the last few years, enrollments in classical humanities courses in a variety of American colleges have been gradually increasing. More recently, there have been several calls for enriching school and college liberal arts programs through introducing students to artifacts from cultural traditions and situations remote from their own, in the spirit of Robert M. Hutchins' observation that "a classic is a book that is contemporary in every age." Both are signs, I think, of a kind of inward-turning in search of values by which we can learn to live serenely in a turbulent world.

The older humanities/general education tradition of my college days had its limits, of course. But for the gay student it may have had special advantages unavailable through present-oriented social science courses and programs highly touted as "relevant" during the last couple of decades. The best of the earlier programs exposed the unsuspecting undergraduate, at least in a limited way, to Greek philosophy and literature. Either through assigned or collateral reading, the gay or lesbian student could thus discover a world in which same-sex commitments were valued and supported. Paradoxically enough, the "positive role models" and values of Socrates and Sappho were considerably more "relevant" to the needs of those students than anything found in canned courses in marriage and the family or abnormal psychology or whatever else kept lesbians and gays invisible or put down in the college curriculum.

In my undergraduate days, available translations of the classics were not as frank about same-sex relationships as they have since become. Most students were exposed to Plato through the translations of the nineteenth century Oxford don Benjamin Jowett. According to his biographer, Geoffrey Faber, Jowett was probably homosexually inclined. Feeling homosexual behavior to be depraved, however, Jowett remained celibate and fudged his translations to spiritualize all forms of gay love. Thus he translates *orthos paiderasteia*, "the right kind of pederasty," as "true love." One sympathizes with gay poet and classicist A. E. Housman's acid comment on "Jowett's Plato: the best translation of a Greek philosopher which has ever been executed by a person who understood neither philosophy nor Greek."

Happily, today's translators no longer follow Jowett's approach to the task at hand. Thanks to them and to such books as K. J. Dover's *Greek Homosexuality*, Royston Lambert's biography of Hadrian and Antinous (*Beloved and God*) or the novels of Mary Renault and Marguerite Yourcenar, anyone with access to a decent library can find positive treatments of same-sex relationships in ancient times. Even books for the armchair or the genuine traveller reflect this new openness. Here's a rather risqué example.

On the Aegean island of Santorini are the remains of the Dorian city of Thera. In its large square, we are told, nude boys danced the *Gymnopaidia* and sang hymns in praise of Apollo Karneios at his annual festival. "From the numerous inscriptions on the rocks around the square," says the learned archaeologist who wrote the text of my guidebook, "we learn that the dances were watched by spectators who could hardly contain their enthusiasm at the sight of the strong, supple bodies of the youths. Frequently in these inscriptions some of the onlookers expressed their admiration for the corporal virtues of their beloved young man."

Lawrence Durrell's charming travel book *The Greek Islands* is a bit more blunt about one or two of the Thera inscriptions. One of them depicts what Durrell terms "a highly serviceable-looking phallus," beneath which is the ambiguous inscription "To My Friends." The other was found on a site on the promontory dedicated to Zeus. It reads (in Durrell's translation) "On this holy spot, sacred to Zeus, Krion has consummated his union with the son of Bathycles and, proclaiming it proudly to the world, dedicates to it this imperishable memorial. And many Thebans [Therans?] with him and after him have united themselves with their boys on this same holy spot."

Of course I don't expect that particular inscription to appear in the assigned reading for Western Civilization 101. Nor is it altogether likely that, when the philosophy class gets to Diogenes the Cynic, the professor will necessarily quote Diogenes' quick response when asked where he had found good men in Greece: "Good men nowhere, but good boys at Lacedaemon."

When I read my first Greek play in high school my teacher certainly didn't direct me to this anecdote, recorded by Hieronymous of Rhodes, concerning its author: "Sophocles lured a handsome boy outside the city walls to consort with him. Now the boy spread his own cloak on the grass, while they wrapped themselves in Sophocles' cape [which, we are told, was of finer material]. When the meeting was over the boy seized Sophocles' cape and made off with it. Naturally the incident was much talked of; when Euripides learned of the occurrence he jeered, saying that he himself had consorted with this boy without paying any bonus . . . ."

Well, that's all chit-chat, of course. But my point is that gay students won't learn these tidbits or any deeper insights into that sex-positive culture which they might adapt in their own lives unless at some point they are encouraged to dig into classical materials. I agree with classicist A. R. Burn, writing in *The World of Hesiod*, that the Greek ideals of "Know Thyself" and "Nothing Too Much" are rather better guides to life than "Thou Shalt Not." That particular insight is especially important for the mental health of lesbian and gay persons. And really to appreciate it one has to tackle the Greeks on their terms, in their wholeness.

In spite of all efforts to constrain or deny it, or to pass it by as "irrelevant" in the contemporary curriculum, the mythopoeic and ethical message of the classical world's artists, thinkers and chroniclers cannot but break through to us, however limited our formal background in ancient history and culture. Part of that message is that same-sex relationships are O.K., that they are inherently capable of satisfying our best aspirations toward virtue in daily living (*arete*). Their beauty and excellence can still be realized in the very different circumstances of the here and now because they represent universal, trans-historical human feelings. Like Krion of Thera twenty-five centuries ago, that is the truth we proclaim proudly to the world.

M. Renault Remembered (1984)

Mary Renault, the lesbian writer, who died on December 13, 1983, was one of my favorite historical novelists. Yet in commenting about her death to two gay male friends, each of whom reads gay fiction, I was astonished to discover that neither had ever read her works, which have given me so much pleasure and intellectual stimulation.

I can't remember when I read my first Mary Renault novel, but it was well before they started coming out in paperback. I began by picking up the earlier ones in used bookstores. I now have most of her books, including the early, so-called "English" novels, one of which, *The Charioteer*, is a gay novel much worth reading. I periodically re-read the "Greek" novels. This past year I even worked her non-fiction *The Nature of Alexander* into a course, discovering that only one student had ever read anything of Renault's before that.

Both my gay friends and my students are missing something. That something is an evocative, authoritative reconstitution of the probable life of Bronze-age, archaic, classical and Alexandrian Greece in which gay relationships are treated as a matter of course. Since that message is presented in such insidiously convincing terms, it is hard to believe that anyone could emerge from a serious reading of it and still see gay expression *per se* as "abnormal," undesirable, or less than fully human.

Renault's eight "Greek "novels are not uniformly good, of course. But in the best of them she brilliantly combines the novelist's imaginative eye with mastery of relevant literary and archaeological evidence. Some of the work is also informed by her special knowledge of medicine and disease, for she trained for three years as a nurse and served as one during World War II. Having read English as an Oxford undergraduate, she had also studied Latin, but taught herself Greek. Renault also travelled extensively in the areas she writes about, thereby being able to interpret the details of her sources and the logical movements of her characters within the context of living landscapes. All these qualities make her very special as a historical novelist.

The first "Greek" novel is *The Last of the Wine* (1956), which many think one of her finest. It is certainly a tour de force, since in it she manages to replicate in English the style of the original Attic Greek. The tale is set in the Athens of Sokrates, and brings to life again many of the characters one meets in classical literature, including Xenophon, the young Plato (with his beloved Aster), and Phaedo. It was, indeed, not until I read Renault that I learned that Phaedo, after whom Plato's magnificent dialogue describing the death of Sokrates is named, had earlier been a slave, forced to work as a "rent-boy" in a gay bathhouse. The narrator, Alexias, is fictional; Renault uses this device in many of her novels. But he becomes the beloved of Lysias, another Platonic character. The central theme is Alexias' growing up through Sokrates' teaching, and through the gay experience, as well as his experience of Athens in war and defeat.

This was followed by a pair of novels based on the legends associated with Theseus: *The King Must Die* (1958) and *The Bull From The Sea* (1962). In the first, Renault brilliantly describes the last days of Knossos. Spurred by it, I started to read the archaeological materials and, last June, visited Crete myself to look at Knossos, as well as the volcanic island of Thera whose explosion may have helped to destroy it. The second volume treats the love of Theseus for the Amazon leader Hippolyta, and the tragic death of their son Hippolytos, falsely accused of rape by Theseus' Queen, Phaedra. I'd known the story from reading Racine's *Phaedra* in college, but Renault's novel, which makes Hippolytos a healer, led me into the literature on Asklepios and Greek methods of natural and psychic healing.

With *The Mask of Apollo* (1966), Renault moved out into Magna Graecia, into the world of the now aged Plato and his former pupil (and beloved) Dion of Syracuse in Sicily, and into the Greek theatre. The fictional narrator in this case, Nikeratos, is a gay actor who travels around Greece and Sicily at critical points in their mutual histories. Some think this is one of Renault's less successful novels, but it stimulated enough interest in me to result in some further reading. I plan to spend a week in Sicily, including a look at the Greek theatres in Syracuse and Taormina, when I go abroad again this spring.

The final part of *The Mask of Apollo* introduces the youthful Alexander of Macedon. In addition to her non-fictional *Nature of Alexander*, in her last years Renault produced a trilogy of novels retelling the Alexander story in a series Gore Vidal has called "one of this century's most unexpectedly original works of art." The first was *Fire From Heaven* (1969), which many think her best after *Last of The Wine*. Second was *The Persian Boy* (1972), "narrated" by Bagoas, a real historical figure who was successively ganymede to Darius of Persia and to Alexander, and it is one of my own favorite Renault novels. Her last book, *Funeral Games* (1981), published when Renault was 75, describes the collapse of Alexander's empire and the obliteration of his family and his hopes. I found this one, like Marguerite Yourcenar's *The Abyss*, to be so depressing that I have been unable to get through it a second time.

Between the last two books of the Alexandriad, Renault turned to a much earlier period, archaic Greece. Her slender novel *The Praise Singer* (1978) is perhaps the most underrated and may be the least known by gay men. It is set in a time when the oral recitation tradition is giving way to writing; indeed Simonides, the lyric poet and the "narrator," helps the Old Archon, Pisistratos, in his recension of the *Iliad*. Although Simonides is not gay, several characters are, including the Old Archon's son Hipparchos, and Aristogeiton and Harmodios, the two young lovers who kill him after Hipparchos has repeatedly attempted to seduce Harmodios.

David Stein has written an excellent appreciation of this novel in the May, 1979 *Christopher Street*. Stein points out that Simonides, at about eighty and living in Sicily, is really giving us an oral history of the bright days of Athens forty and more years before. In the process Renault miraculously makes us hearers, rather than readers. *The Praise Singer* gave point and added meaning to my own rambles around Athens, both on the actual sites and in the museums whose great collections of archaic kouroi are wonderfully replicated in the present-day Greek youths hanging around Constitution Square.

There are many ways to get our story across to ourselves and to the general public. Mary Renault has done a great work for us in her elegant depictions of the gay experience at a level accessible to a literate general audience. If you are one of those gay persons who have not yet discovered her novels, then by all means stock up on these books (most are in paperback) for bedtime reading on these long, cold winter nights. And, yes, it's permissible to read them to each other!

Thebes: The Untold Story (1986)

Seven-Gated Thebes! Today a nondescript modern Greek town of about 16,000 people, huddled atop and around the acropolis of one of the mightiest of ancient cities. Unlike that of Athens, the name of Thebes resonates only tragedy, darkness, evil and suffering, and whatever beyond these is conveyed by Euripides' *Bacchae*.

In legend, Thebes was founded by Kadmos of Phoenicia, who with his brothers had come to Greece in search of their sister Europa, who had been abducted by Zeus in the form of a white bull. Zeus had brought Europa to Crete, where she bore Minos. But Kadmos and his brothers scattered, planting cities where they went. Kadmos settled in Boeotia, where he founded Kadmeia (later the Theban acropolis) and introduced the alphabet and writing to Greece. But Kadmos also offended Ares by killing his sacred dragon, and from then on all kinds of tragic happenings began to happen in Thebes.

The most famous of the Theban kings, the legendary Oidipos (Oedipus), is known to us most fully through the surviving plays of Sophocles. The theme has drawn the attention of creative artists from Aischylos to Gide, including Freud, who fixed on our own culture a new image of this tragic, ultimately self-knowing man. As everyone knows by now, Oidipos killed his father, married his mother Iokaste (Jocasta), and had four children by her, including two worthless sons and one faithful daughter, Antigone.

But in the stories of Thebes we learned in school, the gay parts got left out. How many of us ever heard that Laios, King of Thebes and father of Oidipos, had run off with a beautiful youth before he met Iocaste? Laios had inherited Thebes while still a child, and for his own safety was brought up by King Pelops in the Peloponnese. As a young man Laios fell in love with Pelops' beautiful bastard son Chrysippos, and abducted him while teaching the youth how to drive a chariot. Laios then took his beloved to Thebes and assumed the throne, but soon afterwards Chrysippos was either killed by his legitimate brothers or took his own life. In this way Laios brought same-sex love to Thebes.

Another Theban legend is that of Heracles (Hercules), who was born there and married a Theban princess. As kids, we all heard about Heracles the Hunk, the strong man, the sexual athlete, just the opposite of us sissies who were attracted to other boys. Heracles, like Errol Flynn, did a lot of swashbuckling and slept with a lot of women. But we were never told that, like most good Greeks, Flynn and Heracles had their boy friends as well.

There was Hylas, the beautiful youth drowned by a nymph on the expedition of the Argonauts. There was Abderos, killed and partly eaten by the carnivorous mares of Diomedes, which Heracles had been commissioned to bring back from Thrace. And there was Iolaos, who helped Heracles kill the Hydra and later protected his family. Iolaos and Heracles were "role-models" for gay lovers in Thebes, who swore oaths of fealty to each other at the shrine of Iolaos.

The blind Tiresias, who twice changed his sex, was a Theban seer. The gay poet Pindar lived in Thebes, and wrote of Boeotian lovers. Plutarch, a Boeotian, says that the Thebans were like the Spartans and the Cretans in love and war; all three fought hard and loved youths. Xenophon of Athens observes with some disapproval that "among the Boeotians, man and boy live together, like married people," unlike the Spartan style of male friendship he admires for its restraint. In Plato's *Symposium* Pausanias claims that in Elis, Sparta, and Boeotia there was a simple rule of male love: "It is good to gratify a lover, and no one, young or old, would say that it is disgraceful."

Aristotle describes the sanctuary Thebes gave to the lovers Diocles and Philolaos the Bacchiad, who gave Thebes laws encouraging same-sex relations. Simmias and Kebes, Theban lovers and students of Pythagoreanism. were present at the deathbed of Sokrates and play a prominent role in the Platonic dialogue which describes it, the *Phaedo*. When in Athens Plato's circle was reassessing same-sex love to de-emphasize its physical aspects (the notion of "platonic" love), Thebes clung to older ways.

In the fourth century B. C. the ideal of male pair-bonding was renewed in Thebes with the formation of the Sacred Band. This was an elite fighting unit, sort of like the Green Berets, but made up of picked pairs of lovers who would fight to the death before dishonoring each other by seeming cowardice. Their most celebrated battle was their last, that of Cheronaeia in 338 B. C., when the Band was wiped out by a corps led by Alexander of Macedon, later "the Great." (Alexander's father, King Philip, had been held in Thebes as a youthful hostage, and apparently developed there that taste for young men which later figured in his assassination.) The Sacred Band were buried in a common tomb, marked by an eighteen-foot high marble lion, restored to its plinth in 1904 and still one of the most remarkable of surviving ancient outdoor sculptures.

From Cheronaeia onward, the history of Thebes is all down hill. An anti-Macedonian revolt after Philip's death was savagely put down by Alexander, who demolished the city except for its temples and Pindar's house. Twenty years later Thebes was rebuilt, then sacked again under the Romans. The Greek geographer Strabo reported it as no more than a village in the first century A. D. , and a century later the traveller Pausanias noted that only the acropolis was inhabited. Thebes was successively overrun by Goths, Bulgarians, Norsemen, and Turks, and in the 19th century levelled twice by earthquakes. It would seem that the curse the Gods laid on Kadmos, or Laios (as in Sodom, for the sin of abuse of hospitality, not for homosexuality), or Oidipos, or all three, remained to haunt this unfortunate place.

In the last twenty years or so Greek archaeologists have made significant discoveries in Thebes, though most of their opportunities wait upon excavations for the foundations of new buildings. The ruins of Pindar's home have not yet been identified, nor has the shrine of Iolaos. When and if these things happen, Thebes will once again be in the news.

When that occurs, we shall see whether such august publications as *The New York Times* will mention the fact that Laios and Heracles and Pindar and Aischylos and Sophokles and Euripides and Chrysippos and Hylas and Abderos and Iolaos and Simmias and Kebes and Sokrates and Plato and Phaedo and Aristotle and Diocles and Philolaos and Epaminondas and Philip and Alexander and all their friends (except Xenophon) did things with men the *Times* doesn't think fit to print. Just remember that you read it here first.

Antique Casts (1974)

Marguerite Yourcenar's *Hadrian's Memoirs* is one of those remarkable works of sensitivity and imagination through which the remembered and recorded past is quickened into life. Neither quite a novel nor quite history, the work is a beautifully written meditation on the past and on the human condition, cast in the form of a memoir by the second-century Roman Emperor Hadrian. It is also a powerful, at times agonizing evocation of the love which two men, widely disparate in age and status, can share with each other.

We know little of the history of the aging Emperor's lover, Antinous of Bithynia. Hadrian, a champion of classic Greek ideals of form, may have been attracted not only by the fifteen-year-old's stunning physical beauty but also by a mysterious melancholy Eastern quality which persists in the surviving representations of him. The Emperor, beginning the relationship in his mid-forties, enjoyed five years with his beloved in what Mlle. Yourcenar calls "the long accumulated tradition of heroism, devotion, and even wisdom, with which Greece has ennobled love between friends." Then the boy committed suicide by drowning himself in the Nile, either in self-sacrifice to prevent some mysterious force from harming Hadrian or in the hope that in so doing he would bind the Emperor to him forever.

The stricken Emperor lacerates himself for "the blind self-content of a man too competely happy, and who is growing old." He tries to sublimate his grief by building new cities bearing Antinous' name, one of them near the site of his favorite's death. Hadrian's astrologers tell him that a new star rose at the hour of the boy's death; it is still called Antinous. The Emperor's enormous energies and talents are poured out in commemorating this son-surrogate whom he establishes as a divinity, "that god who every boy dying at twenty is for those who have loved him." The Antinous cult lasted well beyond Hadrian's death, spreading throughout the Empire and enduring some three centuries. The boy-god became a special object of veneration among the weak and the poor, who found in his worship something of lasting beauty, nobility and sadness to which they could respond.

What is left are dozens of statues, reliefs and coins, products of a minor artistic renaissance signifying a root stimulus beyond mere Imperial patronage. A color reproduction of one of these, in Heinz Kahler's *The Art of Rome and Her Empire*, is before me as I write. The damaged statue, from the museum at Delphi, is life-sized. The body is Apollo-like, but the face is that of a particular human being. "The statue of the youth glows for one last time with a radiance like that of the setting sun," says Kahler, and indeed even in small-scale photographic reproduction the flawed image is tantalizingly beautiful.

Dying, Antinous lives. His life is documented only in fragments, many of them negative accounts by early Christian leaders who condemned the openly homosexual origins of the cult and found in its theme of vicarious suffering and death a too close rival of their own seemingly safely asexual cultic figure. Yet Antinous is accessible to us, as gays and as humans, through the works of art brought into being by the acts of his creative, reflective lover.

Hadrian's ideal of beauty was more than mere aesthetics. Beauty was creating cities whose inhabitants were strong and attractive, just and free. Beauty was the elimination of "dire poverty and brutality," and the establishment of justice. Beauty was devotion, useful learning, self-sacrifice, harmony. And beauty is Antinous and Hadrian, loving each other in an ideal symbiotic relationship of intense and trusting youth to wise and caring maturity.

NOTE (1989): A decade after this essay was written, there appeared a fine book by the late Dr. Royston Lambert, *Beloved and God: The Story of Hadrian and Antinous* (1984), containing all the historical background one could wish and a good selection of photographs, many of them images of Antinous artifacts.

I. Romans Noble and Ignoble (1977)

In our preoccupation last year with the Bicentennial of the American Revolution, some of us missed the fact that 1976 marked some other historical milestones, among them the 1900th birthday of the good gay Emperor Hadrian and the 1500th anniversary of the "Fall" of Rome. Coincidentally enough, 1976 was also the Bicentennial of Vol. I of Edward Gibbon's magisterial *History of the Decline and Fall of the Roman Empire*, first of six tomes which view the celebrated Fall as stemming from a collapse of moral values. In spite of scholarly challenge, that interpretation persists among the semieducated to this day, and emerges periodically as yet another weapon against the repeal of the sodomy laws.

If Anglo-American parochialism is indeed a mental disorder of sorts (though like gay King Ludwig's castle-building mania, sometimes a splendiferous one), then the canny curators of our local treasure-trove, the Museum of Fine Arts, are currently providing a magnificent cure. "Romans and Barbarians," a special exhibition which began in December, 1976 and continues through February 27th, 1977, brings together for our enjoyment nearly 500 art objects from the Museums' own extensive classical and other collections and from the precious stores of the Louvre, the British Museum, Oxford University, and at least a dozen other major and minor European and American repositories.

The visitor begins at the height of Rome's power, the second century A. D., and moves through a series of galleries organized spatially and chronologically to illustrate the diversity of the Roman artistic impact on Western

Europe, the Near East, and North Africa - regions which both contributed to Roman art and adapted to it. The Christians and other barbarians infiltrate and invade, and art is placed at the service of the supernatural and liturgical. The Byzantine East evolves independently, the Arabs and others triumph, and art records it all like a barograph. A last gallery shows the continuing inspiration of Roman themes in Western art, including an engaging 1718 Delft porcelain bust of the Emperor Caracalla, Pannini's panoramic plethora of paintings entitled "Views of Rome," and, not least, Mr. Gibbon's very own gold watch, dress sword, and snuffbox. (Not to mention the copy of the first edition of Vol. I once owned by lesbian poet Amy Lowell.)

Of course I was especially interested in items with a gay referent, particularly a marble bust of the aforementioned Hadrian, one of my culture heroes, found in the Nile delta and purchased by the Museum in 1975. Rather surprisingly, there is no representation of his star-crossed lover, Antinous. But there is a limestone statue of a 4th century woman excavated from the site of Antinoöpolis, founded by Hadrian on the banks of the Nile whose waters had claimed the youth in A.D. 130. Hard by the bust of Hadrian is one in red granite of his successor, Caracalla, builder of the famous baths, brutalistically modern in its ambience.

In a case in the second gallery I envied the Musée Alesia its four-inch bronze "Dying Gaul" from the first century A. D. Its aspect is as fresh as though it had been cast yesterday, and altogether I should judge it as one of the most beautiful representations of the ideal male body, live or artistically recreated, that it has ever been my privilege to admire. And of course there were banks of coins from the reigns of, and sometimes depicting, various gay Emperors: the sublime Hadrian; the bestial and sometimes transvestite Caligula; Nero (the original "flaming queen"); the talented and short-lived Titus, who in his salad days had a thing for young male dancers; the "aggressively bisexual" Commodus, who is alleged to have kept a six-hundred person harem, divided fifty-fifty between genders; and others of lesser note.

Gay history aside, there is something here for everybody; textiles, pottery, 177 coins, bronze lamps, jewelry, crosses, buckles, metal and stone sculpture, capitals of columns, even papyrus. May a non-professionally trained art watcher name a few favorites? One is a Romano-Egyptian portrait of young man done in tempera on a wood panel, surviving all the way from A.D. 230. It is especially remarkable for its haunting brown eyes, so very similar to those of my own lover. Another is a seated silver dancer (female) from late fourth-century Greece who leads one directly from Antiquity to Degas.

The same case contains a pair of gold earrings with intaglio, inscribed in Greek "how beautiful," and indeed they are. There are some interesting representations of animals, especially a second-century Tunisian mosaic showing a she-ass nursing two lion cubs, and a sarcophagus with two stylized lions contentedly gnawing away at the necks of two terrified horses. The treasures of the barbarian invaders impress one mostly by their unfamiliarity, but the diadem of the Huns can stand with anything in the exhibit.

A few months ago it took a ruling by the New York State Division of Human Rights and a new Human Rights law to prompt New York's Metropolitan Museum to adjust its membership fee structure to accommodate new life-styles, straight and gay. Our own Museum of Fine Arts' definition of "family membership" reads "husband and wife or two individuals living at the same address," meaning (for our purposes) resident lovers; A. Younger Gay and I became members under that rubric with no questions asked.

To me that symbolizes the difference in tone between the two cities; here in Boston, at least in our cultural institutions, we do things rather more quietly, yet in the classically elegant style which this marvelous exhibit so well exemplifies. So rejoice once more, even in this winter of our climatic discontent, that you are alive and well and gay and living in Boston. And go, too, and see "Romans and Barbarians." It is an event.

Un-Mitigated Gaul (1987)

In 1984 I spent a pleasant month in the West German city of Trier, in the Mosel wine-producing district. The Riesling grape has been grown there for wine-making purposes for more than two millenia. Indeed, my stay coincided with the 2000th anniversary of Trier's foundation as a Roman city, and during my time there I attended numerous exhibitions and musical performances marking the occasion.

The city is full of Roman architectural remains, including a magnificent city gate, the Porta Nigra; the ruins of two sets of baths; and parts of the Emperor Constantine's palace, now a Protestant church. It is also full of medieval, Baroque and Rococo buildings, in spite of heavy Allied bombing during the Second World War.

Trier gets its name from the Treveri, a tribe who by linguistic evidence were mainly Celts; Caesar's *Gallic Wars* contains the first known reference to them. The Romans could not decide whether the Treveri were Germans or Celts or Belgians. But for administrative purposes they formed a part of the Roman province of Belgian Gaul, a motley district between the Seine and the Rhine including what is now northern France, Luxembourg, Belgium, southern Netherlands, and southwestern Germany.

The Gauls were of great interest to ancient writers, partly because they were so different in height, religion and customs, and partly because they were believed to be so similar in sexual preference. Caesar discovered among the Aquitanian Gauls a military force not unlike the Theban Sacred Legion. The Aquitani group of six hundred warriors was made up of pairs of "comrades" committed fully to each other. They shared everything they had in life, and should one lover lose his life in battle, the other was obliged either to get himself killed in the same engagement or to take his own life.

Athenaeus tells us that although the Gauls "have very beautiful women, [they] enjoy boys more; so that some of them often have two lovers to sleep with on their beds of animal skins." Speaking of another Gallic tribe, the Cimbrians, Diodorus reports the same phenomenon and adds that whenever male Gauls are approached by other men, they "prostitute to others without a qualm the flower of their bodies." They did not regard it as disgraceful to yield, we are told, but rather disgraceful to withhold their sexual favors.

In his treatise on astrology, the *Tetrabiblos*, the geographer Ptolemy ascribes the custom of homosexual love among the northern and western Europeans to the influence of the stars and planets governing those territories. "They are without passion for women," he writes, "but are better satisfied with and more desirous of association with men." Aristotle, Strabo, Posidonios and other Greek writers also attribute to the Gauls a predominantly homosexual orientation.

While in Trier I gave some lectures in the local university, which had been established during the Renaissance, suppressed by Napoleon, and refounded in 1970. On my first day there I was guided around campus by an absolutely stunning graduate student in his early twenties. That evening he came by to escort me to a nearby professor's house, to which we had been invited to drink wine and watch the sun set over the Mosel. It was a lovely evening, made more beautiful by the vision in open shirt and denims seated beside me.

About eleven the party broke up, and the student escorted me home through flower-scented pathways; like the English, the Germans are fantastic gardeners. I would have invited him up to my room for a nightcap, but he had previously phoned a person both he and the professor referred to as his "friend," arranging to have the friend meet him at the intersection across from the house where I was staying. When we got there he said I should not bother to wait with him, though I should have found that no imposition. Looking out through my bedroom window, I saw that his "friend" was not another student roomie, but a somewhat older man with a mustache and a Mercedes.

Of course "friend" in German ("freund") suggests something closer than what we normally mean in English. I had sensed from the first that "special" aura about the student; such works of art do not go uncollected for long. I went to bed full of the finest Mosel wine, but unlike the Gauls did not "tumble with a catamite on each side." That night I would have settled for only one.

I also spent a few days in Cologne, another center of the Roman province of Belgian Gaul. Next to the wonderful Cathedral is the modern Roman-German museum, and I was eager to see both. Walking about the city I discerned a gay ambience in the flea markets (of course!) being held in the old market squares, in the clientele going in and out of the bars around the Alter Markt, among the other visitors to the city's superb art museums, and of course along the riverfront promenade where everyone goes for an evening stroll and some look for company later on.

Most remarkable was the railroad station, through which I had to pass any number of times to get to and from my hotel. It was always full of adolescent and older hustlers obviously available or openly making arrangements with johns while the rest of the busy terminal traffic flowed about them. Sunday morning, having ample time before my train, I was browsing in the station shops and became quite aware that the rule here was "ever on Sunday" as well as during the rest of the week. Indeed, a raven-haired beauty in tight black corduroys...but I digress.

It appears that in parts of Gallia Belgica they keep up the most distinctive of their ancient customs beautifully, if perhaps nowadays more commercially. Diodorus is often criticized for exaggeration, but his line about the Gauls' willingness to "prostitute to others without qualm the flower of their bodies" can be empirically verified in any major Gallo-Roman city even at the present day. Who was the kill-joy who claimed that "history is bunk"?

Part Two:
Continental Sophisticates

Learning to Look (1987)

In the January, 1987 issue of *Art and Antiques* (which *Time* calls " a sort of cultural airline magazine") there appeared a new theory concerning Leonardo da Vinci's well-known Mona Lisa. Author Lillian Schwartz claims, on the basis of a computerized comparison with a Leonardo self-portrait, that the final model for the painting was the artist himself. She also asserts that her findings comport well with earlier arguments that the original sitter "may have been male, and that da Vinci may have been a homosexual."

Historical proofs of homosexuality by computer? I must confess that I am no more taken with the argument than the several art historians and curators who have dismissed it out of hand. Even if Leonardo did use a youth as the original, or worked in his own features (neither practice uncommon in Renaissance painting), this is fairly slender "proof" of his homosexuality. That evidence is in any case ambiguous, resting heavily on an anonymous charge that at age 24 he had sex with a 17-year-old hustler. Leonardo was tried for sodomy, but the charge was dismissed. (Then there is the matter of his apprentice "Salai," but that's too much to get into here.)

Of course the creativity of the Italian Renaissance was fueled by the rediscovery of classical models, including models of same-sex affection. It is increasingly well demonstrated, I think, that homosexuality and bisexuality were integral to Italian humanism, the cultural context in which Leonardo, Michelangelo and other artists worked in Rome, Florence and elsewhere. Donatello, Botticelli, Cellini, Vasari, Bazzi (better known as "Il Sodoma") and others were either known to have or suspected of having relations with "boys and beardless youths," in Vasari's phrase.

Nor was that penchant limited to artists. In 1494 the monk Savonarola appealed to the Florentine priests to abandon "your concubines and your beardless youths," and especially "that unspeakable...that abominable vice." (Presumably the one "not to be named amongst Christians"; some of us have to practice it in silence.) Yet when Savonarola was overthrown four years later, one member of Florence's ruling Council of Ten observed to a colleague, "Now we can practice sodomy again."

It's one thing, of course, to try to reconstruct the social history of homosexuality in the Renaissance, as historians such as Guido Ruggiero and Judith Brown have done. It's another to apply serious art-historical and interdisciplinary methods to visual arts subjects of homoerotic interest or intent, though of course art historians have written about heterosexual eroticism in art for years. To merge biography, social history, art-historical methods and contemporary gay consciousness in a viable approach to the homoerotic past is an even more formidable task.

Yet that task is beginning to be tackled, nowhere more impressively than in James Saslow's *Ganymede in the Renaissance: Homosexuality in Art and Society*, published last year with copious black and white illustrations by Yale University Press. Having known Jim for more than a dozen years, and greatly admiring his qualities of mind and taste, I began his book with a sense that I was hardly qualified to keep up with what looked to be a rather specialized sort of analysis. But the argument is clear and well-expressed, and the book well worth the reading even if one is not especially knowledgeable in art history.

Ganymede, in legend, was a beautiful Trojan prince abducted by Zeus to be his cupbearer and beloved. In Michelangelo's day, Ganymede was an icon filled with idealized erotic meaning, used even in religious art. (Saslow's analysis of Michelangelo's representations of Ganymede is extraordinarily well-done.) By the mid-sixteenth century, the sexual element declines in Ganymede's imagery, as open homoeroticism in the culture yields to religious and civil repression and increasing intolerance of homosexuality. A century beyond that, Ganymede has become a symbol of "unnatural vice," and in the hands of Rembrandt has been transformed from a sexy, idealized adolescent to a de-eroticized, squalling, urinating baby. In the end, Ganymede was either dismissed as a subject for serious artists or transformed into the astrological symbol of Aquarius. (As in "the Age of . . .")

The cultural reasons behind all this, the use of the theme by heterosexual artists to tap a homosexual market, the relation of the Ganymede theme to misogyny, and a great many other ideas and insights are among the bonuses of this important book. Jim's current project is an annotated translation of Michelangelo's poetry, also for Yale. Michelangelo wrote a number of very personal sonnets to a young man, Tommaso de Cavalieri, about whose relationship with the artist historians have long debated. After Michelangelo's death the poetry was "edited" by a nephew and published. All of the male pronouns in these particular sonnets were changed to female, reflecting the crackdown on homoerotic experience in that later period.

Although we are living in a more open time, to a large degree the general public is still fixed on negative images of gay people, often based on historical ignorance. There has been too much silence from professional historians on the relation of alternative homoerotic relationships to culture history. Thus there is a long-range significance to such books as *Ganymede in the*

Renaissance, a new edition and translation of Michelangelo's poetry, John Boswell's forthcoming volume on medieval "gay marriage" rites, and other seemingly arcane works of critical scholarship.

These books and others, recently published or waiting in the wings, have begun to yield a tapestry of ideas and concepts which, first influencing other writers and scholars, will gradually filter out into the larger society. There they may work to undermine the walls of ignorance and prejudice which have misrepresented the lives and contributions of homoerotic women and men in other times than our own. And in the doing of it, we in our own time can only benefit, and be thankful.

Venice Re-Observed (1985)

One of the most amusing novels I have read in recent years is Sarah Caudwell's *Thus Was Adonis Murdered*, originally published in 1982 and now a Penguin paperback. I am no great reader of mystery novels, but this one held my attention from start to finish because of its engaging prose style and sharp academic wit. The "narrator" is a middle-aged legal historian at Oxford who potters around with a recherché tome which never seems to get finished, a situation with which I can readily identify. Two of the other principal characters are a dour Scots sculptor and his lover, Ned, described variously by other characters as "one of the loveliest things anyone ever saw," as "something of a flighty piece," and as a subject worthy of Michelangelo or Praxiteles.

Although most of the cerebral activity takes place in London, the murder itself occurs in Venice while several of the characters are there on an Art Lover's tour. Venice has a long-standing reputation as a mecca for gay men. One thinks, of course, of Thomas Mann's novella *Death in Venice* (more recently a Luchino Visconti film), in which the aging Gustav von Aschenbach finds a measure of wish-fulfillment in the aesthetic and sensual contemplation of the youthful Tadzio. And in the late 19th century it was not uncommon for gay expatriates to enjoy the favors of an often happily married Venetian gondolier, such as John Addington Symonds' friend Angelo Fusato, among many others.

Now comes a fascinating book by the historian Guido Ruggiero of the University of Cincinnati entitled *The Boundaries of Eros: Sex Crimes and Sexuality in Renaissance Venice*, published earlier this year by Oxford

University Press as the first in its projected "Studies in the History of Sexuality" series. Ruggiero has made a detailed examination of the criminal records of Venice in the 14th and 15th centuries in order to trace the line between what sexual expression was unacceptable to the Renaissance elite and, by inference, what it perceived as "normal" sexuality.

The very form of the record is important testimony to the biases of that elite since, though most sexual offenses were tried before a Council of State known as "the Forty," sodomy was not. In the 14th century, sodomy cases were heard by a special three-man court, and during most of the 15th by the dreaded "Council of Ten," the supreme ruling council which, until that time, had treated only cases involving high treason and conspiracy against the state. This placement suggests a social meaning for homosexual activity saying less about the act itself than about the fears of Renaissance society.

Renaissance Venice was undergoing rapid social and territorial expansion. The older social disciplines of family and peer control seemed not to be functioning so well, in the face of the new strains put on both individual and society. An increasingly centralized and authoritarian government moved to fill the perceived gaps with new laws and institutions to "protect" family and community. As a result, Ruggiero argues, two sexual milieux emerged: one a "normal" or "licit" culture centered on marriage and the production of children in families, and the other an illicit culture, less well structured but clearly evident, which lay "outside the boundaries of accepted Eros." This culture included fornication, adultery, "crimes against God" (that is, sex with priests, nuns, Jews, or in holy places such as churches), rape and, of course, sodomy.

Sodomy was the most feared of the sex crimes. Its punishment, death by public burning, was in marked contrast to the mild penalties imposed for others, such as the two-year imprisonment for fornication with a nun, a "crime against God." Although "sodomy" included anal intercourse with women and animals, most of the cases dealt with homosexual anal intercourse or its simulation by emission between the thighs of a male partner (or "safe sex" technique, as it were). The "passive" partner, especially if young, commonly got a lighter penalty or was allowed to go without punishment. But "active" sodomites were so feared that in 1467 the Ten required reports of any medical treatment for damage resulting from anal intercourse as a way of tracking down those responsible.

Ruggiero finds in the records evidence of a growing homosexual subculture in the 15th century, suggesting "that homosexuality could become a style and a way of life that it had not been before," especially among the upper classes then being educated in humanism and classical literature.

Certain areas of the city fell under suspicion as "gay turf": schools, barber-apothecary shops, pastry shops, and secluded public spaces such as, for example, the portico of the Church of Santa Maria Mater Domini. Even dinner parties in private homes involving men of differing age groups came to be regulated by the Ten, suggesting both accelerating fears and accelerating realities of the culture of Sodom.

One of the reasons for the creation of a homosexual subculture among upper-class males in Renaissance Venice was deferred marriage, and a consequent lengthening of the period of adolescence; as in classic Greece, Venetian marriages (to much younger women) took place at or near age 30. Same-sex relationships in that period, Ruggiero argues, were often intergenerational and educational. He speculates that they were even an opportunity for younger men to learn the accepted male sex role safely, through first being the more passive partner of an active older man.

The boundaries of Eros in Renaissance Venice were complex, and any brief summary does injustice to Ruggiero's brilliant work. Unlike some of the other manifestations of the culture of illicit sex, sodomy, especially in its primary form of male homosexuality, could not be brought into a functional relationship with the dominant, marriage-oriented culture. Yet even under the wildest rhetorical attack and most barbaric forms of repression, homosexuality in Renaissance Venice blossomed like a rose. "They all set their boundaries," writes Ruggiero, "but Eros, as the Greeks long ago had learned, refused to be limited - perhaps the ultimate proof of divinity." Nobody ever went broke making book on that.

Losing One's Head (1976)

In the absence of role models provided for other adolescents by Hollywood or other contemporary media, the young gay person may gradually assemble his/her own list of "famous gays" and find reassurance in the notion that one can be gay and "important" too. There are problems with this approach to history and identity, but if one is willing to risk finding out that in some cases these reputed gays weren't, and in others that they were behind the door when brains were being handed out, the exercise has its value.

I am more intrigued by the fact that historical biographers are beginning to deal more openly with their subject's sexuality and its individual and social consequences. Such an approach provides us with the chance to go beyond mere name-dropping to learn more of the dynamics of gay and human relationships in contexts other than those available to our diverse but time-bound selves. As Philippe Erlanger's *The King's Minion: Richelieu, Louis XIII, and the Affair of Cinq-Mars* (1972) illustrates, that can be an instructive if chastening experience.

Louis XIII was a harsh, uptight, ailing, guilt-ridden monarch who had married to perpetuate the Bourbon line and ceased even his minimum marital duties after his Queen had finally produced two live-born sons, the future Louis XIV and his brother "Monsieur," (who has been called "France's most notorious seventeenth-century swish"). The eighteen-year-old Henri d'Effiat, Marquis de Cinq-Mars, was maneuvered into the post of Grand Master of the Wardrobe by the crafty Cardinal Richelieu, who had discerned the thirty-seven-year-old King's dominant sexual preference, even though Louis himself had never acted upon it and would not "come out" homosexually for another year. Cinq-Mars was an amoral, vain, flamingly heterosexual Adonis who was perfectly willing to bed the King at Richelieu's behest in order to gain honors and influence at Court. His sexual energy was such that often, after Louis had dropped off to sleep, Henri would gallop from St. Germain to Paris and spend the night with one of his mistresses, returning in time to be present when the King arose and dressed.

Erlanger traces four years of an often stormy and demeaning relationship, during which Cinq-Mars (a rather stupid youth, withal) took his status as the King's favorite a bit too seriously. He broke with his sponsor, the Cardinal, and even dreamed of replacing him as the King's chief advisor in matters of state. Henri also joined a conspiracy headed by the King's brother, Gaston D'Orleans (who also shows up on lists of "famous gays") to overthrow Richelieu, restore the power of the nobility vis `a vis the King, and make a secret peace treaty with France's enemy, Spain.

The outcome was a treason trial set up by Richelieu; the King, as ever stoic and masochistic, refused to intervene. Just as the King had lost his head to Cinq-Mars' tender mercies in 1639, so Cinq-Mars lost his head to the King's justice in 1642. The encounter was equally fatal for all three parties. The ailing Cardinal spat blood and died less than two months after Cinq-Mars was beheaded. The King's depression and grief over his betrayal weakened his resistance to chronic tuberculosis, and he expired eight months after his former favorite.

Erlanger sums up Henri as "a typical adolescent of his class who shared the aspirations of his kind to excel in battle and to conquer beautiful women," who was "made a bait and lured into a trap which also caught the

King and the Cardinal." A fair statement, but it also needs to be said that Cinq-Mars entered the trap willingly, deliberately inducing a highly volatile gay relationship with complete disregard for the older partner's feelings and emotional state.

Yet it takes two to tango, and on his part the King was a smothering, uncommunicative, jealous lover, retaining fundamental feelings of guilt and self-hatred even after he had publicly acted on his homosexual inclinations. Louis XIII was victimized, to be sure, and the whole country took the consequences. But he also set himself up for one classic model of an intergenerational gay relationship, the emotionally and financially exploitative kind which today might be indicated in those classified ads beginning "Young attractive GWM seeks well-established older male for financial support in return for services...."

I'm increasingly convinced, even in these days of monolithic bureaucracies and major economic and social upheaval, that at the individual scale we choose our own fates. A pair of neurotics (gay or straight) who are a sociologist's dream dyad from the standpoint of matched age, class, etc. will proceed to create a joint neurosis because in some perverse way it "feels good."

Contrariwise, cries of "father image" or whatever notwithstanding, gay individuals of the most diverse pairings can and do create new and worthwhile lives together under the most improbable circumstances. It's all in the head; the important thing is that, unlike Cinq-Mars, we avoid bringing about situations where the head and the body end up flying off in two different directions.

One final "relevant" item for the adventurous. According to the gossipy Tallemant des Réaux, an acquaintance entered Cinq-Mars' bedchamber one evening to discover him "being rubbed from head to foot with oil of jasmine. He got into bed.... A second later there was a knock on the door. It was the King. It would seem he was oiling himself for combat." (Note: check local apothecary re ability to supply oil of jasmine!)

An Old Spanish Tale (1986)

The history of crime and punishment is important to anyone interested in gay history, since often the only traces of same-sex relationships, at least for ordinary folk, are those contained in criminal and penal records. Recently I was delighted to discover some of these traces in Mary Elizabeth Perry's *Crime and Society in Early Modern Seville* (1980), which I found while browsing in a Boston bookstore's remainder section.

Ms. Perry's argument suggests not only how "criminal justice" operated as a system of social control by male leaders of the church and state, but also how lawmen and crooks need (and perhaps deserve) each other. While she disclaims any definitive statistical base, she uncovers some intriguing detail on homosexuality in a Spanish city in the 16th and 17th centuries which probably has general usefulness. Her most important single source is a record kept by a Jesuit priest, Fr. Pedro de Leon, concerning the prisoners he saw as a prison chaplain from 1578 to 1616.

Among those convicted of sodomy in this period in Seville were two schoolmasters and five priests. It appears that priests were especially prone to sodomy and counterfeiting (as further evidence in municipal and church records suggests), while soldiers, for example, preferred rape, robbery and murder as their capital crimes of choice. Fr. De Leon acknowledges that sodomy was considered a serious disciplinary problem in both priests and monks. One cleric was punished by the Inquisition for using the confessional to solicit young boys. And a fellow Jesuit told Fr. De Leon that there were no problems over women with his fellow clerics, "because they had many young male students and novices with whom they could sin."

The nobility, too, seemed to contemporaries especially prone to homosexuality. Preachers criticized the sons of the nobles for their idleness, sensuality, "effeminate" appearance (as marked by long, curled hair and the wearing of plumes), and general depravity. Often the erring noble was made an example of, especially in cases of murder or sodomy, in a kind of trickle-down deterrence theory. In 1597 one Alonso Telles Giron, who was connected by blood or marriage with just about all of the nobility of the province, was convicted of murdering his wife. On the King's orders, Giron had originally been sentenced to strangulation in private rather then the more humiliating, if similarly fatal, public hanging. However, when Giron confessed also to numerous acts of sodomy, he was re-sentenced to public burning along with one of his male partners, to the presumed delight of a rather large crowd.

Perry observes that a very high proportion of those receiving capital punishment were executed for sex crimes. Fr. De Leon reports sixty such cases, of which only two were for adultery, four for rape (a hanging offense), two for bestiality, and the remaining fifty-two for sodomy. One of the men convicted of bestiality was burned (the punishment for sodomy), though his sex partner, a burro, was hanged. Perry argues that both the numbers and the method of execution suggest that sodomy was feared not simply as a "sin against nature," but as a threat to the political and moral order jointly enforced by King, Church, and municipality.

Female sexuality was largely controlled through the institutions of marriage, the convent, and the licensed brothel. Female prostitution was sanctioned by the state through the establishment of municipal brothels. The minimum qualifications were to be an orphan and neither a virgin nor of noble birth. The social control of females extended only imperfectly to lesbians, however, described in some accounts (written by men) as women wanting to be men. The evidence of "manly" behavior, interesting enough, was not only the fashioning of dildoes, but the lesbians' use of what was once called "gutter language" and their habit of strutting around and crowing like roosters.

There was, of course, much more social ambivalence about the employment of boys in the sex trade. Some became pimps for their sisters or girl friends, or went into the business for themselves. (It would appear that hustling has always attracted free-lancers.) But Fr. De León records the existence of at least one "house of play" in which young boys, "painted and elegant," were available for hire. The twist concerning this particular establishment is that, though every patron was committing a capital crime, the house was kept by a sheriff.

Those outside the Establishment did not have the same entrepreneurial opportunities as this lawman, however. In 1585 a Negro was accused both of sodomy and of the procurement of young boys for sex. He found himself dressed up in lace ruff, curled wig and painted face, and along with two other youths similarly decorated was paraded through the city, presumably by way of warning, both to themselves and to the other citizenry of Seville.

Perry's findings match those of other historians (such as Guido Ruggiero on Renaissance Venice and Alan Bray on England in the same period) in finding homosexuality to carry a freight of fear and subversiveness enormously out of proportion to the nature of the rather private acts involved. It's really pretty bizarre, when you think about it. When I was young it used to be said that gays were sick, but I can't think of anything sicker than straights in power going into a frenzy over gays wanting to make love in ways which are natural for them without having to take on the whole extra load of legal or discriminatory baggage as a consequence.

Yet straights will still go into sick frenzies, seemingly at the slightest provocation, and here is Perry's other cautionary item. She finds that increased official prosecution of gays is strongly related to increased "puritanism" in social attitudes. In our own day, we seem to be experiencing such a neo-puritan threat as the radical religious right gains in political influence, though most Americans do not (yet?) share their specific social attitudes. History never, of course, repeats itself precisely, but it does set before us potentialities and precedents which it would be foolish to ignore. "He who has ears to hear, let him hear."

A Neglected Lesbian Artist (1984)

Lesbian history and biography, until recently, has been less well cultivated and less widely known than it deserves to be. Yet the intense archival, community, historical and biographical labors of lesbian and non lesbian women in the past few years hold promise of redressing that matter. The endnotes in Lillian Faderman's *Surpassing the Love of Men* (1981) and the bibliographic entries contained in Margaret Cruikshank's edited volume, *Lesbian Studies: Present and Future* (1982) are greatly useful guides to further reading and suggest the surprising amount of work accomplished thus far.

Recently I picked up a copy of *Rosa Bonheur: A Life and a Legend* (1981), by Dore Ashton, with photos selected and informative captions written by Denise Browne Hare. Back in the Dark Ages, when I was in grammar school, I was given a set of color reproductions of great European paintings. I held on to them for a number of years, and one that I remember distinctly was Rosa Bonheur's "The Horse Fair." While living in New York after college I saw the original, which was donated to the Metropolitan Museum in 1887 by Cornelius Vanderbilt. Of course when I was a kid I didn't know anything about her life, and I certainly didn't know she was lesbian; at that age and time, who knew what a lesbian was, anyway?

Dore Ashton's book proved a useful antidote to my artistic and biographical ignorance about Rosa Bonheur. Bonheur was the daughter of an artist and teacher of art who had faith in his child's greatness and encouraged her to become an artist herself, in spite of the tradition of visual art as a male preserve. Early on she became interested in animals and, like Landseer in England, she was to make her mark primarily as an animal painter. Raimond Bonheur, her father, was a Saint-Simonian and a strong believer in the abstract equality of the sexes; as often happens, this was not always reflected in his home life. It was actually a Jansenist priest friend who prompted Raimond to send his daughter to the boys' school he ran, along with her two brothers. The experience both of studying with boys and of playing "boys' games," she later wrote, "emancipated me before I knew what emancipation was."

In effect, Rosa had to crack a man's world on male terms. You are invited to take your choice as to whether or not she therein gained a feminist consciousness; Ashton and Hare say she did because of her successful insistence on equality, while Faderman says she didn't because she male-identified. Most of the time she dressed in boyish or men's clothing, which certainly made sense, since so often she was drawing or painting barnyard animals from life. Though her dress was seen by innocent contemporaries as a little peculiar, modern psychological labels like "transvestism" had not yet risen to limit the freedom of someone like Bonheur to choose the manner of dress with which she felt most comfortable.

At the age of fourteen Bonheur became friends with Nathalie Micas, a former pupil of her father. Friendship ripened into life-long commitment, until Nathalie's death in 1889. Bonheur took on the role of protector of the sickly Nathalie, and in turn Nathalie picked up the household management chores, which freed Rosa to paint. Publicly, of course, Bonheur described their relationship as "sisterly," in an age when lesbians were still depicted as horrid monsters. As Faderman says of the period, "the likes of Rosa Bonheur and Nathalie Micas, who were certainly lesbians and certainly not - aside from Rosa's genius - a unique couple, were nowhere to be found in French novels of the day." Of course nowadays it is too easy to dismiss their division of labor as "role-playing" or "butch-femme stereotypes." It is really only important, it seems to me, that we acknowledge this to be a loving same-sex relationship, and this the authors of *Rosa Bonheur: A Life and a Legend* do, quite matter-of-factly.

Through Nathalie's support and her own talents, Bonheur was able to become a distinguished painter of animals, to achieve economic and social independence and even to buy a chateau (still standing, but somewhat derelict) at the edge of the Forest of Fontainebleu. Rosa and Nathalie could thus live quite happily, independent of any need for a supporting male cast. One day, annoyed by the facetious comment of someone who had seen her out riding with a newly married male acquaintance, Rosa snapped back that "the fact is, in the way of males, I only like the bulls I paint." My sense of it is that she did indeed realize that in this male-defined society she was still under constraints, even though she had proven herself artistically and economically.

After Nathalie's death, Rosa's physical and mental health declined somewhat for about a decade. Yet shortly before the end of her life she found another woman friend, Anna Klumpke. A young American artist whose portrait of Elizabeth Cady Stanton hangs in the National Portrait Gallery in Washington, Klumpke moved in with Bonheur in 1898. Dore Ashton tells us that there is "little doubt of the passionate love she had inspired in the aged painter," who referred to Klumpke in some intimate letters as "my wife." The two women often painted side by side and the Metropolitan Museum in New York has a striking Klumpke portrait of Rosa Bonheur in old age.

When Bonheur died in 1899 she left her entire estate to Klumpke. Bonheur was buried in the cemetery of Père Lachaise in Paris, in the same vault as Nathalie Micas. In 1945 the vault was opened once more, to receive the ashes of Anna Klumpke. In the nineteenth century there were few more open ways of at last publicly acknowledging "special friendships." It sounds lugubrious to say so, but in those days it was "out of the closets and into the tombs."

Ironically enough, Fontainebleu's monument to Bonheur was a huge bronze bull, a grandiose copy of one of her early small sculptures; it was melted down by the Germans during World War II. Although Rosa Bonheur's artistic fame has faded with the passing of the naturalism she espoused in art, we are fortunate that our understanding of her life has been broadened and made more meaningful for us in this frank and beautiful book.

Freudian Odyssey (1984)

Just seventy-five years ago this month Sigmund Freud came to Massachusetts, accompanied by Carl Jung and three other European psychoanalysts. Pausing in Boston only long enough to change trains, they went on to Worcester for a week's stay. There, before a gathering of American psychologists and psychiatrists assembled at Clark University,

Freud delivered a summary of his teachings, the so-called "Five Lectures on Psychoanalysis," and Jung first publicly set out his concept of "introversion."

Three-quarters of a century later the Freudian movement seems hip-deep in slogans, accusations of malpractice, suggestions of "cooking" the documentation, and hints at skullduggery of whatever sort. Women's groups remind us of the unfortunate phrase "anatomy is destiny," and of Freud's exasperated query to his disciple Marie Bonaparte (H.R.H. the Princess George of Greece), "What do women want, anyway?" (At minimum, one would think, to be known as Marie Bonaparte, psychoanalyst, in preference to H.R.H. the Princess George of Greece!)

Male gays remember equally unfortunate phrases, such as "arrested development," and even more the appropriated omniscience and arrogant domination of a generation of therapists. Following the epic battles of the early 1970's between gay liberationists and the therapeutic establishment, many were tempted to go all the way with Nobelist Sir Peter Medawar in his claim that "doctrinaire psychoanalytic theory is the most stupendous intellectual confidence trick of the twentieth century."

The key word here, perhaps, is "doctrinaire" which, whether occurring in left-wing politics, right-wing economics, old-consciousness theology or new-consciousness liberation movements, is perhaps the current cultural ailment most in need of therapy. In any case, we can scarcely with justice blame Freud for the sins of a therapeutic establishment whose most homophobic members, such as Irving Bieber and Charles Socarides, come out of an analytic school which rejects Freud's core idea that all humans are to some degree constitutionally bisexual.

That aside, let's commemorate Freud's American visit by looking back at some scraps from his life and times which indicate varying attitudes toward homosexuality. Thanks to Laura Z. Hobson's novel *Consenting Adults*, which quotes it, many gays know about his sensitive letter to the American mother of a gay man who wrote Freud in 1935 asking for help. In his reply, Freud told her that homosexuality was "nothing to be ashamed of, no vice, no degradation". He also said that it wasn't even an illness, but rather a variation of the sexual function which her son shared with many "highly respectable individuals of ancient and modern times," some of whom he lists.

In words which should have shot the ground out from under the doctrinaires, Freud denied that most homosexuals could change their orientation through therapy. Therapy, he claimed, could replace conflict over sexual identity with harmony and peace, whether or not change occurred. In other words, therapy could, at most, help unhappy homosexuals to become happier ones. But it could not legitimately be used to try to change unhappy homosexuals into heterosexuals.

Freud was in the right place to study sexuality and its variants during his early and middle years in Imperial Vienna. The Imperial family itself had its lavender brigade, which included the Emperor Franz Josef's youngest brother, Archduke Ludwig Viktor, who was so blatant that at one point he was confined to a rural castle and guarded entirely by female attendants. In the memoirs of Cynthia Sternberg, an Austrian noblewoman, there is brief reference to a celebrated scandal of her youth in which "two well-known young aristocrats had been caught making love in the men's lavatory at the jockey club." (No doubt the jockeys were busy with the horses.)

The American anarchist Emma Goldman, discovering that Freud's lectures at the University of Vienna were open only to physicians and other special students, registered with a professor who also lectured on sex, in order to qualify for later admission to hear Freud. In Professor Bruhl's course she heard about "Urnings" and "Lesbians" as well as "other strange topics." In her memoirs she describes her classmates as "a peculiar assembly" of "feminine-looking men with coquettish manners and women distinctly masculine, with deep voices." The passage suggests the presence in this large city during the 1890's of an educated population of lesbian and gay folk who were searching for self-understanding as well as the general cultural significance of human sexuality and its repression.

Freud's correspondence with Jung and others demonstrates his interest in homosexuality and his acquaintance, not always positive, with individual homosexuals. In June, 1909, he wrote Karl Abraham that Magnus Hirschfeld, the well-known German gay rights advocate, was "certainly an agreeable colleague because of his well-sublimated homosexuality." But when Hirschfeld broke away from the Freudian movement in 1911, Freud described him to Jung in rather different terms. "No great loss," writes Freud. "He is a flabby, unappetizing fellow, absolutely incapable of learning anything." He ascribed Hirschfeld's departure to "homosexual touchiness." In responding to Jung's inquiry concerning Herbert Silberer, who had just submitted a paper to him on the interpretation of dreams, Freud describes the author as "an unknown young man, probably a better-class degenerate." (I've always thought of myself as a better-class degenerate whose development has never been successfully arrested.)

Freud was, in some sense, a patron of gay history. Just after he returned from America he wrote his famous study of Leonardo da Vinci which was, I think, the first bit of Freud's work I ever read. Other psychoanalysts followed; a Swiss disciple, Oscar Pfister, published a similar study of Count Zinzendorf, founder of Moravian communities in Central Europe and at Bethlehem, Pennsylvania. (Add Zinzendorf to your list of gay "founding fathers.")

Like anyone who wrestles with an intractable intellectual problem over a very long period, Freud was sometimes right, sometimes wrong, sometimes inconsistent, sometimes rigid. But his attempts to weigh the individual in the balance of nature and culture, to see us as biosocial beings with a need both to manage and to express whatever sexual orientation is appropriate to us, are rather more relevant to current intellectual trends than they have been for some years.

Near the close of his American lectures Freud put that need for balanced expression in terms gays will appreciate more than most. "The claims of civilization make life too hard for the greater part of humanity," he observed. "We ought not to go so far as to fully neglect the original animal part of our nature, we ought not to forget that the happiness of individuals cannot be dispensed with as one of the aims of our culture."

Procession of Boys (1983)

Earlier this fall the distinguished and outspoken ballet star, choreographer and director Sir Anton Dolin returned to Massachusetts for a brief visit to Jacob's Pillow, the dance center in the Berkshires. The occasion was a performance of his one-man theatre piece, "Conversations," which includes reminiscences of the great organizer of the Ballets Russes, Serge Diaghilev, and his star-crossed protegé, Nijinsky.

Sir Anton, born Patrick Healy-Kay in 1904, was a child actor in J.M. Barrie's "Peter Pan" and, in 1921, became an "extra" in the Ballets Russes production of "Sleeping Beauty" - chosen by Diaghilev, Dolin says, because he was pretty. He returned to the company in 1924 as the premier danseur in "Le Train Bleu," with libretto by Jean Cocteau and music by Darius Milhaud. Later, Dolin was to be acclaimed in two Balanchine ballets, "Le Bal" and "The Prodigal Son," in the last year of the Diaghilev company.

Dolin falls in the middle of what a *Boston Globe* interviewer calls a "procession of boys" whom Diaghilev developed into great dancers in the teens and twenties of this century. With a directness which is perhaps unusual even in the 1980's, the *Globe* interviewer asked Dolin if the tales of the master's offstage relationships with his protegés were true. Dolin's response seems to me an extremely revealing one in the midst of a statement intended to reveal nothing: "So much of what is published is fictitious. Life was much simpler and much nicer in those days. It wasn't so open and vulgar."

Dolin was somewhat more forthcoming about the allegedly simpler life with Diaghilev a few years ago when he was interviewed by Richard Buckle for the latter's massive biography, *Diaghilev* (1979). As a former member of the corps de ballet, Dolin certainly knew Diaghilev's erotic preferences, and indeed had been sexually awakened himself quite early, having as a boy in Ireland been seduced in the confessional by the local priest. In any event, at the age of 19, in November, 1923, he moved into Diaghilev's sleeping compartment of the train en route to Monte Carlo. What was far more important, Dolin became one of the four major male dancers whose substantial yet unformed talents were spotted by the master and nurtured by him personally and professionally, to the great benefit of the dance world of our century.

You'll have to read Buckle's biography of Diaghilev to get the measure of this many-sided man. Neither dancer, nor musician, nor visual artist himself, Diaghilev had the special talent of being able to bring all three together to innovate and to educate. As Dolin says of him, "his great talent was seeing talent in others." Born in Russia, and always interested in bringing Western European art to Russia and bringing Russian art westward, he had been actively gay since the age of eighteen, when he and his cousin, "Dima" Filosov, had become lovers. While preparing to bring his first group of Russian dancers west for the 1909-10 season, the thirty-five-year-old Diaghilev was introduced to Nijinsky by the latter's current lover and patron, Prince Paul Lvov, who then diplomatically bowed out. Buckle's earlier biography, *Nijinsky* (1971) elaborated that encounter, as did Herbert Ross' extraordinarily lovely film "Nijinsky," all too briefly shown in Boston two or three years ago.

Diaghilev rehearsed with Nijinsky an initiation rite which was to occupy the last twenty years of his life. First he would identify a great potential talent in a teenaged boy, and bring him in for a period as lover-companion-pupil. Then he would present him to the world with those talents extraordinarily made over into real professional competence, allowing some space (but not enough) to grow under his aegis. The relationship would break off as the beloved moved on, not only in professional development but sometimes in sexual orientation as well.

Diaghilev's inability to let go was perhaps the only real flaw in the process. The Nijinsky story is too well known to bear repetition. His successor, the eighteen-year-old Leonide Massine (who looked in profile, we are told, like "one of the ripening boys whom Baron Von Gloeden photographed at Taormina") became a great dancer and choreographer under Diaghilev's patronage. But in 1921, Massine was dropped by the master when, like Nijinsky, he fell in love with a female member of the corps de ballet. A month later Diaghilev found the seventeen-year-old Russian exile Boris Kochno who, after a brief relationship, stayed on as an artistic collaborator in the Ballets Russes.

Dolin, whose twentieth birthday in 1924 was celebrated in Venice and marked by the master's gift of a copy of Thomas Mann's *Death in Venice*, was also too independent in the long run for the possessive Diaghilev. One of the more amusing examples of the problems in their relationship is the story Buckle tells of the time Dolin went swimming with two lesbians. He was then charged by the jealous Diaghilev with having an affair with one of them, an accusation which must have startled (and later amused) all three swimmers. In any case, by 1925 the twenty-year-old Serge Lifar, whom Diaghilev had discovered in 1923 but put on the back burner, had replaced Dolin as the reigning favorite.

In spite of quarrels and difficulties, this seems to have been one of the easier examples of Diaghilev's late relationships. For one thing, there was clearly no danger of Lifar's going off with a woman. Buckle retails another anecdote about a German fan of Lifar's who managed to insert herself surreptitiously into his bed. When Lifar awoke to find her there, he promptly threw her out, but the scent of Chanel No. 5 remained. So before Diaghilev came in for the night, Lifar had to break his own bottle of the same substance in the bath to avoid having to make difficult, if truthful, explanations.

Such a tale suggests that Dolin's characterization of life with Diaghilev as "much simpler" might be questioned. But Buckle's evidence suggests and Dolin's testimony confirms that at their best these relationships were indeed exceptionally "nice" ones and very far from "vulgar." Diaghilev, of course, was not always in control of his own feelings, but there was a genuine interest in feeding the minds and raising the aspiration levels of his protegés. He made sure that they read good books, talked with the best contemporary musicians, artists, literary and cultural figures, and visited museums and old churches with him as guide. Dolin calls him a "great educator," and he was, both in leading out what was already in his pupil, and in adding to that process what used to be called liberal learning. Dolin's statement that Diaghilev "could charm a diamond out of a lump of coal" perhaps sums up the technique.

Diaghilev's last relationship, with a sixteen-year-old student of Nadia Boulanger, future composer and conductor Igor Markevitch, was a late and self-giving idyll. Markevitch, who is not gay, reminded Diaghilev of the young Massine. For perhaps obvious reasons, Buckle steps round the question of whether there had been some physical expression of that relationship. But the most important part, as Markevitch recalled, was Diaghilev's generosity and his mentoring role. Like earlier protegés, Markevitch was taken to galleries, operas, music festivals and fine restaurants. He remembered that Diaghilev had made these boyhood experiences a very happy time for him, even though the master was then terminally ill with the diabetes which, in those days before insulin, was to take his life at age 56.

As we grow older, we are inclined to look back on an earlier day and claim simplicity for it too easily. My own introduction to the world of the ballet came, some years ago, through the briefest of romantic flings with a premier danseur whom I shall not name. (In my day, as in Dolin's, although we may have kissed, we did not tell!) After the usual intimacies, he suggested that I remain for what was left of the night and have breakfast in the morning with him and his wife! I did not then possess the sophistication necessary to carry off that sort of encounter, and bowed out as gracefully as was possible under the circumstances. The memory is a delicious one, but I am left with the sense that, in dealing with the balletic past, complexity is a better model than simplicity.

The relationships of Diaghilev and his protegés were not simple, for both he and his "procession of boys" were or became talented and complex men. But they were nurturing relationships, anything but vulgar, and at their best moments were emblematic of the kind of self-giving which needs to be a part of our own relationships, of all kinds. They may not have been as open as are many in our own day. But the historical record of such gay relationships is something of which we can, I think, legitimately and equally be proud.

NOTE (1989): Sir Anton Dolin died in Paris on November 25, 1983.

Part Three:
"But We Don't Do That; We're British!"

A King's Minion (1986)

> The mightiest kings have had their minions:
> Great Alexander lov'd Hephaestion;
> The conquering Hercules for Hylas wept;
> And for Patroclus stern Achilles droop'd.
> And not kings only, but the wisest men.
>
> Christopher Marlowe, *Edward II*

Echoes of Evelyn Waugh's homoerotic novel *Brideshead Revisited* were heard in June when an Oxford undergraduate, daughter of a British cabinet minister, died after a drug and drinking party. The all-night affair was thrown in the Christ Church College rooms of Count Gottfried von Bismarck, a descendant of the famous 19th century German chancellor. Young Bismarck is a member of what one press report called "one of the notorious university dining clubs that Waugh depicted in Brideshead," the Piers Gaveston Society.

Who was Piers Gaveston? More notorious than the Society named for him, he was the flawlessly beautiful lover of the Plantagenet King Edward II (b. 1284), who ruled England from 1307 to 1327. Gaveston was a Gascon squire who, having fought with distinction under Edward's father, had been appointed companion to the young prince. "And when the King's son saw him," wrote one chronicler, "he fell so much in love that he entered upon an enduring compact with him." What began as an adolescent "crush" for a handsome bravo turned into the real thing. But early in 1307 the old king, fearful of the problems this relationship might cause for his son's forthcoming marriage with a French princess, banished Gaveston from England.

Gaveston departed in May 1307, but the ailing King died in July. The new King, now an extraordinarily handsome 23-year old, immediately recalled Gaveston, made him Earl of Cornwall (a royal domain, now held by the Prince of Wales), showered upon him many other honors and properties, and married him to one of the royal nieces. The English nobles were inflamed by Gaveston's insulting remarks and the King's excessive generosity, especially when Gaveston turned up at court wearing jewels from the young Queen Isabella's dowry. It became a matter of common gossip that the King preferred Gaveston's bed to that of his own French bride. The barons revolted in 1308, and civil war was averted only by the King's sending his lover to Ireland as Lord-Lieutenant.

Gaveston was recalled in 1309 after concessions by the King, but the barons persisted in trying to get rid of him permanently. Exiled a third time in November, 1311, Gaveston was back and being publicly entertained by the King at Windsor before Christmas. The following year Gaveston was captured, imprisoned in Warwick Castle, and subsequently murdered by the nobles. "His chief offense," writes Edward's biographer, "was his lack of respect for the great barons of established lineage, little culture and less wit...."

The King's grief was extravagant and so were his cries for vengeance. Rebellion and defeat in Scotland, civil war in England, and invasion from France under the now estranged Queen and her lover, Roger Mortimer, followed over the next dozen years. Edward was captured in November, 1326 and deposed in favor of his young son, Edward III, the following January. Imprisoned in Berkeley Castle, he was murdered there on September 21, 1327.

A number of lurid tales sprang up concerning Edward's murder. It was said that he died of the effects of having "a hoote broche [a red-hot spit or poker] putte thro the secrete place posterialle" (need I modernize?). Presumably this was to remind him of Piers Gaveston. These stories have been questioned by some scholars, though John Boswell leans toward acceptance in his *Christianity, Social Tolerance and Homosexuality* (1980). One chronicler, a Cistercian monk, complains of "too much sodomy" between the King and Gaveston, and another says they had "a love which is said to have surpassed the love of women," citing the example of David and Jonathan. There is also dispute over the relationship between the King and a later "minion," Hugh le Despenser, some thinking it purely political and others also sexual. Boswell refers to le Despenser as "Edward's second lover" and points out that before le Despenser's own execution (also by the nobles) his genitals were cut off and publicly burned, a common penalty for sodomy.

Edward's elaborate tomb in Gloucester Cathedral, erected by his son (who later executed his mother's lover and shipped Isabella off to an isolated castle in East Anglia), soon became a place of pilgrimage and of reported miracles ascribed to the martyr-king. Edward's tragic story became the subject of a famous play by the gay Elizabethan playwright Christopher Marlowe, whose Edward "frolics with his minion," Gaveston. There is also a less well-known version by Berthold Brecht.

Edward was something of a patron of the arts and crafts, and founded Oriel College, Oxford. During the 17th century the front quadrangle of Oriel was rebuilt, to include a Hall boasting an elaborate porch, over which were erected statues of the Virgin Mary and two of the gay kings of

England, Edward and James I (who had formally incorporated the college in 1603). Later, in the 19th century, Oriel College became a principal base of the Oxford Movement, a somewhat homoerotic affair which led to a devotional and liturgical renewal within the Church of England. This was the start of an Anglo-Catholic religious tradition which has always attracted disproportionate numbers of gay men.

Three years ago I gave a paper before an international conference of scholars at Oxford, and was delighted to find myself housed in Oriel College and dining in Hall under the gaze of its gay kingly Founder. I also amused myself by identifying the gay subjects in the portraits and stained glass windows under the magnificient hammer-beam ceiling of the Hall, in the intervals between lusting after the bod of a handsome young waiter, who one day wore a lavender necktie. (Oh, well, one can dream on... .)

Oriel was the last of the all-male Oxford colleges to go co-ed, though three all-female colleges remain. Nowdays the University's best-known male homosocial hangout is the nude bathing-ground on the Cherwell, "Parson's Pleasure." The area is surrounded by a high fence displaying a sign forbidding "ladies" to pass beyond a certain point. Under the sign, at the time I checked it out, some ardent feminist had spray-painted the words "sexist poseurs." Ah, Piers Gaveston, where are you, now that we really need you?

Room at the Top (1976)

Gays with a taste for history, glitter or scandal will be interested in Lady Antonia (Longford) Fraser's new biography of King James I of England. Ms. Fraser, it may be recalled, has been named by Vivien Merchant, actress and wife of the playwright Harold Pinter, as corespondent in what promises to be Britain's most sensational divorce case since the salad days of the Duchess of Windsor.

The multi-talented Lady Antonia contends that James has been bad-mouthed as a ruler because of the moral judgements an unreflective posterity has made about his private life. In her preface, she warns the little old ladies from Dubuque that the King's "personal predilections followed a course outside the accepted norm." That is classic British understatement; in fact, James was actively homosexual both during his adolescent and his later life.

James, like Frederick the Great, had a hell of a childhood. Starved for affection, at the age of thirteen the Scots King fell for a handsome older French cousin, a young débauché whom James showered with titles and gifts and who in turn used the young ruler's love to advance his own political power. (Ms. Fraser suggests that "had an equally attractive woman come his way at the same propitious moment, the homosexual inclinations of King James might never have been aroused," which I find rather näive.)

Three years later James was compelled by ultra-Protestant Scots nobles to banish his lover to France. Taking his grief out in poetry, the boy-king wrote pathetically

> And shall I then like bird or beast forget
> For any storms that threatening heaven can send
> The object sweet, where'on my heart is set
> Whom for to serve my senses all I bend? . . .

James was conscious of his official duties as a royal stud in a time of succession problems, and in 1589 married a Danish princess with whom he maintained some sexual relationship at least through the conception of the Princess Sophia in 1606. They lived in separate households, however, for ten years before Queen Anne's death in 1619. The Fraser biography does not discuss James' male attachments between 1582 and 1607, but in the latter year (the year Jamestown was founded) the forty-year-old King lost his head to the first of two "fatal favorites," a charming, rather unintelligent Scots teenager named Robert Carr. (Forty is a dangerous age!)

The learned King taught Carr Latin, among other things, made him his private secretary, and elevated him to the House of Lords. Carr (by then Earl of Somerset) eventually went straight and was replaced by the arrogant, corrupt and magnetic George Villiers, whom the King in due course named Duke of Buckingham in public, and his "sweet child and wife" in private. (Yes, that's the same Duke of Buckingham who appears as the French Queen's lover in *The Three Musketeers*; shed a tear for her, for the French King was in love with a boy too.) Lady Antonia rightly criticizes James, not for having male lovers, but for allowing them to accumulate and use political power in a manner contrary to the King's interests.

In 1616 Somerset's newly acquired wife poisoned his best friend (those were parlous times!), and in the backlash from that scandal the King's gay life-style was openly and severely criticized. James' public kisses for his favorites were excoriated as "licentious," and one oft-cited knight (who had been banished from court, to the detriment of his objectivity as a witness) wrote nastily of the King's "slobbering" over his young men, and even accused him of walking around with "his fingers ever . . . fiddling about his cod-piece." Angered by such criticism from those he (rightly) regarded as his inferiors, James (a firm believer in Divine Right) defiantly told his council in 1617 that his attachment to young men followed the example of Jesus Christ: "Christ had his John and I have my George." In an era when Puritanism and placing limits on the King's prerogative were in the ascendant, the analogy didn't play very well.

Lady Antonia's brief book is well written, generously illustrated (including charming depictions of the unfortunate King's rapacious lovers), and grounded in recent scholarly research. And how sweet it is in the year of the Bicentennial, to learn that America's first Chief of State had no qualms either about kissing his lover in public or telling the world to go to Hell when it raised its collective eyebrow.

Bountiful Affections (1977)

A late acquaintance of mine, who was a distinguished historian of science, once wrote apropos of something else that "the paucity of women ... has almost completely deprived the history of exploration of sexual interest." Well, even Homer nods, and I certainly wouldn't hold that statement against his memory. But from what we know of so-called "situational homosexuality," we would have better history if historians of same-sex institutions and activities were more sensitive to the "sexual interest" which surrounds these circumstances like an aureole.

The famous episode of the mutiny on H.M.S. "Bounty" has attracted the attention of naval buffs for nearly 200 years, of history buffs for a slightly lesser period, of fiction buffs since the publication of Nordhoff and Hall's *Mutiny on the Bounty* in the 1930's and of film and late-night TV freaks since Clark Gable and then Marlon Brando played the role of the protagonist-mutineer Fletcher Christian in the two movies made from it. In the first "Bounty" film Lt. William Bligh, the ship's captain, was played, appropriately enough, by Charles Laughton, whose widow has just revealed his own penchant for attractive young men.

The "Bounty's" captain has come down to us as some kind of ultimate in cruelty and brutality; to liken someone to "Captain Bligh" is akin to calling someone an "Attila the Hun." Yet Bligh, in the judgement of modern scholars, was guilty less of brutality than of remarkably poor judgment. And his direction of a 45-day, 3500 mile journey after the mutineers had put him and his loyal minority of followers to sea in an open boat places him among the greatest navigators of all time. (His journal of the mutiny and subsequent escape was sold at a London auction last fall for over $90,000!)

In case you were wondering, it can now not confidentially, and not here for the first time, be revealed that Bligh and Christian were probably bisexual, that it is likely that they were shipboard lovers, and that the famous mutiny, while it had a great deal to do with food and verbal abuse and the discovery of V. D. and chance, also has overtones of homosexual guilt, a lovers' quarrel, and the petulance of an aging bitch when his favored love object starts chasing grass skirts with a scandalous degree of enthusiasm.

Such is my reading, at any rate, of the evidence presented in British naval historian Richard Hough's very readable 1973 book, *Captain Bligh and Mr. Christian*. The gauntlet is thrown down at the close of the first chapter. In addition to being "hated and feared by some but admired by many more, and earnestly and loyally loved by one woman," writes Hough, Bligh "was loved, too, for several years - the most eventful and fateful years of his life - by one man, as emotional, passionate, and mercurial as himself, with whom his name will always be linked - Fletcher Christian."

Bligh had been a protegé of the renowned Pacific explorer Capt. James Cook, discoverer of the Hawaiian Islands, who had taught him nautical surveying and cartography. Bligh later assumed command of H. M. S. "Britannia" for two voyages to the West Indies, taking with him Christian, son of a good Cumberland family Bligh was anxious to please. Bligh, then 31, gave the 21-year-old midshipman quick promotion to second mate for the second voyage. The disgruntled first mate later accused Bligh of showing "partiality for the young man." Through Christian was an indifferent seaman, the mate claimed, Bligh had been "blind to his faults and had him to dine and sup every other day in the cabin, and treated him like a brother...." (Brother indeed!) Christian wrote his own brother that he had found Bligh "a very passionate man, though I believe I have learned how to humor him."

Two years later Bligh was given command of the "Bounty," with instructions to sail to the South Seas both to explore and map unknown areas and to gather breadfruit trees at Tahiti, known through Cook's visit there. The breadfruit trees were to be taken to the West Indies for transplanting, as a food supply for slaves on the burgeoning British sugar plantations. Bligh appointed all his officers, including the fourteen-year-old midshipman Peter Heywood. Christian was made first mate.

The ship reached Tahiti after ten months at sea; once there, the officers and men, except for Bligh, broke their long heterocelibacy "frequently and fervently," to steal a line from Wallace Hamilton's novel *Coming Out*. Christian, after a ritual period of promiscuity, settled down with a female tyo, whom he renamed Isabella. And, says Hough, he "also acquired, as many go them did, a male tyo - a servant-cum-friend." (Bligh's diary records the Tahitians' "uninhibited acceptance of sodomy" and oral intercourse.)

The famous (or infamous) mutiny took place on April 28, 1789, after the ship had left Tahiti and the tyos behind. The causes are multiple, and certainly included Bligh's inept attempts to restore traditional naval discipline after several months of the fleshpots and indolences of Polynesia. It appears that even on Tahiti Bligh had made Christian a sort of scapegoat, often humiliating him in front of his male tyo, who he knew admired Christian greatly. Heywood had also been rebuked in front of his male tyo. The two joined with others, rebels with a variety of causes, and seized the ship, dropping the Captain and a few loyalists off in the ship's launch. The latter, thanks to Bligh's superb seamanship under pressure conditions, reached Australia in a month and Timor, then Dutch territory, by mid-June.

The "Bounty," meanwhile, had returned to Tahiti, dropped off Heywood and others who wished to remain there, picked up several Tahitians of both sexes, and headed eastward to remote Pitcairn Island. Here the ship was burned, the mutineers fell out with each other, and waves of violence and murder decimated the colony. The small band of survivors embraced Christianity and forswore alcohol, raised children whose decendants still inhabit the island, and were rediscovered only in 1808, by a surprised Yankee whaler. The other surviving mutineers had long since been captured and some of them executed. Bligh lived on until 1817, retiring as an admiral.

Hough's last chapter addresses the issue of sodomy at sea in this period, with particular reference to what he calls "the mystery of the Bounty mutiny" and of Christian's parting message to Heywood at Tahiti. His hypothesis is that Bligh, whose role demanded that he remain aloof from the attractive natives and live on the ship, was jealous of the full-blooded heterosexual life Christian was leading on shore. We will never really know, but Hough argues that the most plausible explanation for the intensity of Bligh's bitterness is that "Bligh and Christian had enjoyed for a long period a homosexual relationship, a relationship going back to their first voyage together in 1785."

He argues also that Christian, moving further into heterosexuality, had recoiled from his past and was unwilling to renew a relationship with an older man who had insulted him repeatedly in front of his tyo. The message which Heywood (a close friend) carried to his grave was probably that Christian had been under so much pressure from Bligh to resume sex with him that he was temporarily out of his mind, joined the mutiny, very quickly regretted it, and discovered it was too late to back out. A secondhand charge of sodomy against a married captain as a defense against mutiny charges would not have stuck, and Heywood knew it.

Both Bligh and Christian were highly strung. Christian, always hungry for affection, usually received it because of his charm and exceptional good looks. A "weak, moody, temperamental and sentimental young man," in Hough's appraisal, neither Christian nor his fellow midshipmen (most of whom were appointed for their family influence) could rise to responsibility in the real world when it was demanded of them. And Bligh's nagging and ego-reducing tactics ultimately drove them into joining something they had not started and whose consequences they were unable to anticipate.

The "Bounty" was only in a limited sense a gay cruise ship and its mission more than high adventure. But if Hough is correct, at least part of the darkness surrounding the affair is the situational homosexuality or at least bubbling homoeroticism working on the sensibilities of a rather insensitive commander and a group of immature and virile young studs whose sexual orientation was still "confused" and whose ability to understand themselves and their situation was limited, to say the least. It was, perhaps, a classic homosexual melodrama.

NOTE (1989): Soon after this article was written, work began on a third film version of the "Bounty" mutiny. Titled simply "The Bounty" and directed by Dino DeLaurentis, it starred Anthony Hopkins as Bligh and Mel Gibson as Fletcher Christian. Allegedly basing their work on Hough's book, the film makers sanitized the story of any homoerotic component, and the subject is not even hinted at indirectly. It is another scandalous example of the movie industry's spinelessness in gay matters. In any case, the film itself turned out to be over two hours of continuous tedium which an honest treatment of Bligh's and Christian's complex relationship might have relieved.

Beyond the Statistics (1987)

Earlier this summer the reality of AIDS broke through the statistics for me once more. Within a week's time I had attended memorial services at Harvard for a thirty-year-old professional acquaintance who had died of its effects; learned of the death of a twenty-eight-year-old gay man who had wanted to join our newly formed diocesan AIDS task force but was too ill to attend our first meetings; and discovered that a third person, whom I'd known through Integrity, had died at the age of thirty-five at his midwestern home. It was also the week that Michael Bennett, who wrote a new chapter in the history of the American musical theater with his "A Chorus Line" and other works, died of AIDS in Arizona. That week also eighteen young Mexican men, having crossed the border illegally in the interest of economic survival, were suffocated to death in a railway boxcar near El Paso.

As Edna St. Vincent Millay reminds us in her "Dirge Without Music," the untimely deaths of those younger than ourselves is no new thing: "so it is, and so it will be, for so it has been, time out of mind." But to gay men my age, the loss of "the beautiful, the tender, the kind;...the intelligent, the witty, the brave" of the next generation, now seemingly going down in windrows, outrages one's sense of the natural order of things. "I know," Millay writes. "But I do not approve. And I am not resigned." Neither am I.

If we look at the statistics, however, we learn that until fairly recently annual death rates always reflected disproportionate numbers of the young, especially infants and children. This was so because of periodic incursions of such epidemic diseases as smallpox, cholera, yellow fever, and malaria, as well as of tuberculosis, largely a young person's disease in the 19th century. One such case from gay history has recently come to light, contained in a fragment of the diary kept by a middle-aged gay man, one Edward Leeves, between April, 1849 and July 1850. Leeves was a moderately wealthy British expatriate living in Venice when, in the face of a threatened Austrian invasion during the wars for Italian nationhood, he decided to flee to London for the duration. A week after his arrival he saw a handsome twenty-two-year-old guardsman, and made a date with him after parade the next day.

After several meetings Leeves took Jack Brand "to Albany Street, or one just by," evidently to the Victorian equivalent of a hot sheets place. Here Jack sang for him, and then "he laid his Head, with his beautiful Hair, on my shoulder." A couple of weeks later they spent a four-day holiday in rented rooms, with champagne, at Gravesend, a London outport accustomed to transients, where presumably no one would ask sharp questions. Jack went back to the Royal Horse Guards (that is, "the Blues," part of the Queen's household cavalry) and Leeves went off to the country for three weeks.

They had made arrangements to meet again in London on September 6th. The day before, however, Jack died of cholera, then raging through Europe. He was one of an astounding 6644 persons to die of cholera in London in the month of September alone, the worst single month of the epidemic there. But to Edward Leeves, Jack was no statistic. Rather, in what was apparently a lifetime of gay relations with men in uniform, this was (says his editor) "the most precious emotional experience of his life."

His beloved had no known relatives (and possibly had entered the service under an assumed name), so Leeves buried him in Brompton Churchyard and provided a tombstone. He later tore out the pages of his diary for the days immediately following Jack's death, but the text resumes in mid-December and continues until the end of July, two months after Leeves had returned to Venice. Much of it is lament over what might have been, and a recording of his depressed state as he recalls this "beautiful apparition! ... So young, so beautiful, so gay!" Leeves, too, was not resigned.

Although still mourning Jack, his own life had to go on. By late December he meets "two stunners from Canterbury," and a month later almost picks up a trooper from a Scots regiment. By mid-February Leeves is entertaining more "Blues" at a local pub or in his lodgings, sometimes two at at time. Though sometimes complaining of them as "drunken brutes," he more often praises them: "What a set of fellows these Blues are!"

Leeves then makes connections (evidently commercial as well as affectional) with Jack's best buddy, one Paxton, appropriately nicknamed "Screw," and described as "a bold, audacious blackguard, such as I like." Leeves frequently entertains Screw and another trooper, Tom Roberts (who "do look stunning in their White Leathers"). He even takes Screw to Gravesend, to the same rooms he had shared with Jack. Screw's father buys out his son's contract with the guards so Screw can get married. On his last night in the Blues, Screw visits his patron in full uniform, though telling him he will now have to break off the relationship.

Back in Venice, Leeves destroys his earlier diaries and waits impatiently for letters from Screw, musing that "the gayest and merriest days of his life are, I fear, gone, passed among the Blues." Sure enough, marriage and civilian life do not work out for Screw. By diary's end Leeves has been taken by him for another 200 pounds, supposedly for an investment in England, but which Leeves suspects Screw will actually use to fund a wild goose chase to the gold fields of California.

Leeves' remnant diary was discovered among her late husband's effects by a British widow in Venice in the late 1940's. She gave it to a neighbor, another [gay?] British expatriate, Victor Cunard, who had it typed up for the edification of friends "who he thought might appreciate it." One of them was John Sparrow, sometime Warden of All Souls College, Oxford, who found a London publisher for it under the title *Leaves From a Victorian Diary* (Secker and Warburg, 1985). Although in 1849-50 Leeves wished desperately to die and be buried in the same grave as his beloved, (a Victorian post-mortem "coming out" ritual; Cardinal Newman did the same thing with his beloved), he survived Jack by more than twenty years.

Queen Victoria would not have believed, much less approved, what was going on with her Household Cavalry. Who of us, knowing better (through no doubt approving), would have believed that this pathetic fragment of one middle-aged gay man's encounter with love and unpredicted death would survive at all? And yet it has surfaced in the 1980's as a kind of indirect reflection of our own concerns in these, the "cholera years" of our own lifetimes.

Paradise Ungained (1983)

Arthur Charles Benson was the eldest of five gay offspring (three sons, two daughters) of Edward White Benson, ninety-fifth Archbishop of Canterbury. Arthur, like so many late Victorians, was a compulsive diarist. He left behind some 180 volumes of diaries, containing approximately five million words. These were were sealed in the Magdalen College (Cambridge) library with instructions that they were not to be opened until fifty years after his death, which occurred in 1925.

Arthur, a well-known essayist and biographer in his day and practically forgotten in ours, is in many ways the nicest and most interesting of all the Bensons, gay and otherwise. Now that his diaries are available to scholars, we can learn something of the inner life of this gay academic who spanned an era in which certain gays came to understand and give a name to their feelings, even if they could not bring themselves to act upon them. It is this portrait of a gay man of that transitional period which seems to me to be the most valuable contribution to gay history made by David Newsome's lengthy 1980 volume *On the Edge of Paradise: A. C. Benson, The Diarist*.

Arthur was, says Newsome, "an interesting figure rather than a person of great historical consequence." He was primarily an observer, not a participant; "his gifts were essentially spectatorial." These qualities made his diaries worth preserving, but they seriously inhibited the conduct of his life. Like many of us growing up gay, he solved his "problem" by holding back, by avoiding intimacy while at the same time hungering for it. He longed for love, yet was fearful of its possible consequences. He stood "on the edge of Paradise" (Arthur's phrase) but was never able to enter its gates.

At age 22 Arthur took a "temporary" post at Eton College, and remained there for twenty years. He was an especially fine housemaster and teacher, perhaps in part because he became so skillful at walking the tight-rope between his romantic need for intimacy (or for a son-substitute) and the realities of his professional responsibilities and his own inhibitions. While at Eton he made a modest literary reputation in biography and essays, and developed a broad range of literary, ecclesiastical and royal acquaintances, through whom he got the job of editing the *Letters of Queen Victoria*. In the fall of 1904, when he was forty-two years old, he was elected Fellow of Magdalen College. Almost immediately he became a kind of father-figure or confessor whom Cambridge undergraduates sought out as a mentor not boxed-in by the narrower forms of erudition demonstrated by many of his colleagues.

As his diary shows, Arthur gradually became more relaxed and honest with himself, recognizing the erotic rootage of his romantic friendships with handsome, aristocratic youths. He rejected the notion of genital sex, however, and decried the grossness of such Decadents as Oscar Browning, Oscar Wilde, and Hugh Walpole (who as a student had come out to him with a frankness which shocked Arthur to the core). At the same time he took an aesthetic and sensual pleasure in the sight and company of the graceful and charming ephebes of his chosen college and university. There survives an interesting letter of Rupert Brooke, whose androgynous magnetism attracted persons of either gender in prewar England, describing "an infinitely affecting tête-à-tête dinner" with Arthur in 1912. "He implored me to write him," reports Brooke. "I nearly kissed him. Both were drunk."

Arthur came out of a background which stressed the classics in education, and in the late 19th century classical study provided one of the few bases for positive feelings about being gay. After uncovering hard evidence that the subject of one of his biographies, Walter Pater, was actively homosexual, Arthur mused in his diary that "if we give boys Greek books to read and hold up the Greek spirit and the Greek life as a model, it is very difficult to slice out one portion, which was a perfectly normal part of

Greek life, and to say that it is abominable, etc., etc." And again, "Isn't it really rather dangerous to let boys read Plato, if one is desirous that they should accept conventional moralities?"

Arthur's romantic friendships continued even after he was elected Master of Magdelene in 1915; indeed, the last of them, with undergraduate George Rylands, occurs only a year or two before Arthur's death at age 63. He talks out his last relationship with his brother Fred (E. F. Benson, the novelist) and with his friend Geoffrey Madan, finally questioning his choice of celibacy and distancing as a mode of coping with his gayness. To Madan he concedes that his upbringing, which made him regard all sexual relationships as "rather detestable" and "a thing per se to be ashamed of," had blighted his outlook. After discussing what he called "the homo sexual question" with Fred in 1924, Arthur commented on the paradox that marriage was considered an honorable estate, indeed a "virtuous duty," while "all irregular sexual expression" was condemned or excluded from consideration. "The 'concurrence of the soul' is the test surely?," he writes. Not quite "if it feels good, do it," to be sure, but certainly a reflection questioning conventional morality in the light of his own gay life experience.

In January, 1905 Arthur wrote in his diary that "I don't think I am an entirely conventional person." Certainly he was not an unconventional person; no Bohemian, no Decadent he. But for that very reason Arthur Benson's gay experience is worth examining since it represents probably the majority experience of those of us who grew up before the present era of support groups and positive gay literature and gay political activism. Absent such resources, one had to find one's way alone through the writings of Plato and biographies of "Great Gays" and one's own feelings in order to conclude that conventional morality in this area was indeed inadequate, and then cope with that realization, again alone, as best one could.

Certainly it is a mistake to think that most gays in the past were either political radicals, aesthetes, criminals, alcoholics or insane German rulers, to name a few standard stereotypes. Most of us were, and perhaps still are, best described in Arthur Benson's phrase, not entirely conventional persons. But then there is that little margin of unconventionality which, as it did in Arthur Benson, may make us gentle questioners of received opinion, ironic observers of men and things, friends of our friends and nurturing mentors of the rising generation. After all, as Arthur says,"to be a Don and not to care, romantically, for the young men [is] a very chilly affair."

Those qualities, and that warmth, are not bad contributions to the flux of human experience. That is why we need more of the kind of documentation and understanding of ordinary but interesting gay lives which books like *On the Edge of Paradise* now bring us.

The Higher Sodomy and the Biographer's Art (1985)

While on a brief trip to Cambridge University a couple of years ago I visited the Fitzwilliam Museum. On special exhibition was a collection of rare books, prints and drawings formerly belonging to one of that university's most gifted scholars, the economist John Maynard Keynes (1883-1946). Keynes' collection includes a number of works by gay artists and others which convey subliminal gay messages. My favorite was a Cezanne, "L'Enlèvement" (1867), showing a gorgeous male hunk in the foreground, lifting a much less detailed female. The hunk's back is to the viewer, effectively concealing most of the woman's body but revealing some very sexy attributes of his own.

Roy Harrod's "official" two-volume biography of Lord Keynes, published in 1951, carefully and deliberately conceals the facts of Keynes' homosexuality, in part in the interest of securing a fair hearing in homophobic America for Keynes' demand-management methods. Michael Holroyd's two-volume biography of Lytton Strachey (1968), however, speaks much more frankly about the role of homosexuality for Keynes and others associated with the writers and artists of the Bloomsbury group. As the last survivors of Keynes' immediate family died in the late 1970's and early 1980's, and as more personal papers were made available, it became much easier to write about Keynes' inner life as well as his public one. Two recent biographies by Charles Hession and Robert Skidelsky tell between them about all there is to tell about Keynes' sexual odyssey.

That odyssey began in the family. Hession argues that "androgynous parents are most likely to develop androgynous children;" that is, the offspring "learn or aquire traits from both parents in some balanced or combined form." Less successfully, Hession also cites the alleged importance of birth-order factors. The argument here is that "the spoiling of the first child may induce homosexual tendencies." Skidelsky tells, however, that Keynes' younger brother and sister also exhibited bisexual tendencies, so we'll just leave that one for the witch doctors.

In any event, in Maynard's case, the successive milieux of Eton, Cambridge and Bloomsbury appear to have sustained his early orientation, which Hession argues very strongly is the key to Keynes' unusual creative ability as a thinker. At Eton he ran with a largely homosexual set. There were the usual platonic schoolboy crushes, but in his senior year also some actual experimentation with Dillwyn Knox (brother of Monsignor Ronald Knox), who later married and fathered two sons, the elder named Maynard.

In his first year at King's College, Cambridge (where he later became a Fellow), Keynes was elected to the Apostles, a twelve-member university-wide secret society which over the years has numbered some of the most eminent English intellectuals. Strachey was then Secretary of the group, and in examining its records had concluded that many of its earlier members had been closeted, non-practicing homosexuals. He termed this stance "the higher sodomy," by which he meant "a sort of ideological homosexuality which manifested itself more in words than in deeds."

Strachey, Keynes and others of their circle began to articulate and elaborate this hitherto implicit "higher sodomy," not simply as a sexual preference but also as an ethical position. They argued (incessantly) that love for or between young men was higher, ethically speaking, than the heterosexual male's love for women. To be sure, there was a misogynist cast to that argument, since under it women were deemed less worthy of the higher forms of love. Still, what Keynes and Strachey were doing was undergirding sexual preference with moral philosophy, and thus articulating a new type of gay life-style.

Of course in that more distant and more shockable era they were quieter about it than modern gay liberationists. But they eagerly joined theory and practice, so much so that Bertrand Russell, an older and non-gay Apostle alumnus, would later assert that after his time, under Strachey's influence, "homosexual relations were for a time common" within that group. Both Hession and Skidelsky document the election of bright, beautiful and seducible young "embryos," as well as the rivalry among some of the current Apostles over those newly elected. Strachey and Keynes broke temporarily over who had first dibs on one "Dicker" Duckworth, described by Strachey as "pink and delightful." (In those remote days it was pink, and not punk, which was considered delightful.)

Maynard's most sustained grand passion was with the Bloomsbury artist Duncan Grant. They were more or less together as lovers for about five years, and remained "best friends" for life. Grant, who was Strachey's cousin and former lover, was an important influence on Keynes' appreciation of contemporary art. Grant later became the lover of Vanessa Bell, Virginia Woolf's sister. Strachey later married heterosexually and in 1925, at the age of 42, Keynes wed the boyish-looking ballerina Lydia Lopokova. He was later to comment that, among the prime objects of his life before World War I, love had been the first by a wide margin. That comment can only be understood in the light of Keynes' experience of a particular form of gay life-style, the "higher sodomy" of Lytton Strachey's coining joined with the physical love of men.

We learn from Hession's book to think of Keynes' life and work in terms of the union of passion and intellect, coupled with the originality of the "outsider's" stance which informs the best of gay writing. We learn from Skidelsky's book the darker facts of how the truths of Keynes' life were suppressed by his first full-length biographer, Harrod, who disapproved of both homosexuality and "frivolous" Bloomsbury. In the interest of historical truth, and not merely in the interest of gay liberation, we must be grateful that Hession and Skidelsky have so fully and so honestly profiled the gay man whose ideas have so heavily shaped the political and economic landscape of our own time.

Radclyffe Revisited (1986)

During the last few years gay organizations both political and cultural have often taken the name of some lesbian or gay male figure as a sort of icon or source of inspiration. Thus we have Harvey Milk and Alice Toklas political clubs, or Djuna Barnes, Gertrude Stein, Oscar Wilde or Walt Whitman bookstores, and even a major archives and library collection named after Natalie Barney and Edward Carpenter. During the same period a number of good biographies have appeared recounting the lives and times of these movement icons.

Yet until recently we have had no decent biography of one who deservedly ranks with these as a forerunner of gay freedom, the British novelist Radclyffe Hall. Hall is best remembered, of course, for her controversial novel *The Well of Loneliness* (1928), which used to be a must reading for any lesbian, though in more recent years *Rubyfruit Jungle* has replaced it as your basic lesbian "coming out" novel. Una Troubridge, Hall's longtime lover, published a memoir entitled *The Life and Death of Radclyffe Hall* in 1961 and authorized her literary executor, Lovat Dickson, to write another, appearing in 1971 under the inane title *Radclyffe Hall at the Well of Loneliness: A Sapphic Chronicle*.

The eighties, however, have seen the rise of what might be called a Radclyffe Hall cottage industry. Claudia Stillman Frank published a study of Hall's novels entitled *Beyond the Well of Loneliness*, Virago Press has issued a new paperback edition of *The Well*, and two biographies have appeared, Richard Ormrod's *Una Troubridge: The Friend of Radclyffe Hall* and Michael Baker's *Our Three Selves: The Life of Radclyffe Hall*. (Curious that both these biographies are written by men.)

Radclyffe Hall was born Marguerite Radclyffe-Hall in 1880, unwanted daughter of a philandering father, Radclyffe Radclyffe-Hall (whose well-deserved nickname was "Rat"), and a vain, spoiled and mentally unstable American mother. Not much is known of her early life, but it seems clear that she was quickly forced to develop her own strong inner resources in order to survive. By her late teens Hall had realized she was "different" in her erotic life. She began writing poetry quite early, and eventually published five volumes of her poems, all before she wrote her first novel. A large inheritance from her grandfather, a wealthy doctor, came to her on reaching her majority, in 1901. From then on, she had the resources to live comfortably and as she chose, to travel, and to follow her own literary bent.

After several early crushes, she fell improbably in love with a married grandmother, Mabel Batten, known to her friends as "Ladye." Batten had much earlier been one of the mistresses of King Edward VII. She and the still awkward and relatively uncultivated Hall became lovers in 1908 and travelled extensively together, setting up housekeeping in Cadogan Square, London after the death of Ladye's husband, until Ladye's own death in 1916. Ladye was a powerful influence on the younger woman, among other things by teaching her to appreciate the style and technique of the English novel.

Hall had a roving eye, however, and had at least two affairs on the side before Ladye's death. The second of these was with a relative of Ladye's, Una Troubridge, then the wife of an admiral and the mother of a child. After Ladye's death Una became the "significant other," though during the course of that 28-year relationship Una had to endure Hall's infatuation with a younger woman, a Russian emigré called Souline.

After some early success as a novelist in the 1920's Hall began to absorb the ideas of Havelock Ellis, who had held the theory that "sexual inversion" was congenital, not something one arbitrarily (and perversely) chose for oneself. If that were the case, reasoned Hall, then the invert could not help him/herself and therefore should not be stigmatized for that condition by society. She determined to write a novel of ideas in which this point of view would be exemplified by a noble and high-minded invert who, like herself, felt society's unfair stigma but in some sense triumphed over it by inner force of character. Nobility and preachiness do not go well in novels, and *Well* suffers from the rhetoric of the soapbox. But the point is, of course, that in the 1920's Hall was gutsy enough to tackle the job.

The furor which publication aroused was kicked off by Lord Beaverbrook's powerful *Sunday Express*, which published a rabid editorial demanding that the book be suppressed under the obscenity laws. Denouncing the book as one which would bring the "plague" and "disease" of homosexuality out into the public arena and thereby increase its incidence, the editorial concluded with the following backhanded testimonial to the power of literature: "I would rather give a healthy boy or a healthy girl a phial of prussic acid than this novel."

Hall and her publisher were haled into court in a celebrated censorship case, which they lost, and lost again on appeal. Many writers and other notable figures came to Hall's defense, most brought in by the censorship issue rather than the literary merits of the book. (Almost nobody beyond Hall and the attorneys for the defense claimed *Well* was a literary masterpiece.) Nevertheless, the book was banned in Britain and remained officially unobtainable there until 1949. But it was published in other countries and translated into several foreign languages. Even by the time of Hall's death in 1943 fifteen years after its initial publication, *The Well of Loneliness* was selling an astounding 100,000 copies a year worldwide.

Under the power of Ladye's example, Hall had converted to Roman Catholicism, and Una was of the same faith. Una was Hall's heir, of course, both to Grandfather Radclyffe-Hall's fortune and the royalties from Hall's books. She moved to Florence in 1949 and then to Rome, where she lived an affluent if remote life-style until her own death in 1963, at age 76. By her will, and in accordance with Hall's wishes, the estate was left to an English Franciscan convent, the Order of the Poor Clares in Lynton, England. Long may their work be sustained by the profits from the book that broke the taboo on lesbian themes in literature!

Paederistic Evangel (1984)

Last year I was privileged to spend ten days in Oriel College, Oxford, where I participated in a scholarly conference and stayed on to explore the treasures of the town. In the classical gallery of the Ashmolean Museum I encountered a Roman marble copy of a late Greek statue (c. 423 B. C.), a lithe and sexy torso of a Greek youth. The inscription read "Given in memory of Edward Warren and John Marshall by Three Friends" (unnamed; the year of the gift was 1932).

To see the name of Edward Warren in Oxford was to be at home again. Edward Perry (Ned) Warren (1860 - 1928) was a gay Bostonian responsible for supplying the initial core of the great classical collections both of

Boston's Museum of Fine Arts and of the Metropolitan Museum in New York City. The son of a prosperous Boston manufacturer, Warren was taken to Europe at the age of eight. There he was brought through various art collections and found, he said much later, that what attracted him were the nude statues, "the male as much as the female." He went on to play out the same-sex side of that early erotic feeling, through grammar-school crushes, adolescent straying from his parent's Calvinism toward the ritual sensuality of the high-Episcopal Church of the Advent, the discovery of Walt Whitman's poetry, and a passion for the writings of the dandyish Boston visitor of his college years, Oscar Wilde.

At Harvard he abandoned his youthful Anglo-Catholicism in favor of salvation through classical art. Two years out of college, he made his first trip to Greece in 1885, accompanied by another gay Harvard man, William Amory Gardner ('84), long a master at Groton School. On this trip Warren purchased his first work of Greek art, a terra-cotta nude youth ("Helios"), now at the Boston Museum. Returning to England, Warren settled into Lewes House in Sussex and remained an expatriate for the rest of his life.

Warren had gone from Harvard to a period of study at New College, Oxford, where he met John Marshall, a Lancashireman who had also forsworn religion in favor of classical studies. Marshall joined Warren at Lewes House as "secretary-companion," and soon there grew up in Lewes a community of bachelor scholars, living in the spirit of Oscar Wilde's England rather than Victoria's, and supported by Warren's share of the income from the family paper mills. Most of the communitarians were in their late 20's or early 30's when the community began. But Warren, we are told, "delighted to take under his wing any boys or young men who, whether promising or not, happened to cross his path." Others enjoyed photographing the local adolescent males of the Lewes swimming-baths, after the fashion of their contemporary Baron Wilhelm Von Gloeden of Taormina.

Beginning in 1892 Ned and Johnny began their career of serious collecting, initially for themselves only. Soon they began collecting for the Museum of Fine Arts and after 1905 they also collected for the Metropolitan. A number of university museums, including Oxford's, later received parts of Warren's private collection as gifts. In a letter of 1916 accompanying a gift of 600 pieces to Bowdoin College, he wrote that a museum of art is "a traitor to the modern cause lodged amid utilities for the succor of renegades . . . . My humble and delightful work is meant for one or two people not yet born." Although Warren believed that "art is inevitably for the few," it seems clear that his own message was directed to an even smaller minority among lovers of classical art.

When Warren began collecting, very few American art museums would display the male nude in any form. The sculpture collection of the Museum of Fine Arts began largely as a museum of plaster casts, and Dr. Henry J. Bigelow, Professor of Surgery in the Harvard Medical School, was asked in 1876 to affix fig leaves to the appropriate parts of the anatomy of the nude reproductions. Today one of the Museum's finest classical works is a grave stele featuring an archaic youth, nude. This was originally bought by Warren as five fragments, and offered to the Museum in 1903. The Curator of Classical Art blocked the purchase initially, because "the lower fragment of that could not be exhibited publicly." Even after it was given to the Museum by Warren's straight brother Fiske, it remained unassembled and unexhibited for over fifty years.

"Johnny" Marshall married in 1907, but the two men remained close friends. Warren fell in love several times thereafter, the last affair coming at the age of 58. His lovers, in true Greek fashion, appear to have been mostly young men; someone once said of him that he would have made an ideal master of novices. He either adopted and/or settled income on several of them, with mixed results. One of them inspired a rush of poems and the early drafts of his privately and partly posthumously published *Defense of Uranian Love*, a gay apologetic which was initially distributed only to close friends and a few major British libraries.

It was not until some thirty years after Warren's death that the classical objects he had scouted out began to be shown as he had wished. In 1964 the erotic vase fragments from his personal collections, which he had given the Museum of Fine Arts in 1908, were finally publicly shown. The Ashmolean is responding even more slowly to the modern world. In an old-fashioned case I spotted a red-figure piece given by Warren himself. Although it is by "The Painter of the Oxford Ganymede," you can't see Ganymede who, the text tells us, is playing his lyre for Zeus as Eros peeps out from behind a rock. That side of the pottery is jammed against the back of the case without even a mirror to show the main theme. All that one sees of the artistry of the "Oxford Ganymede" painter is the safely clothed Athena on the side facing the presumably corruptible visitor.

In later life Warren was asked "whether he gave Greek antiquities to American museums for the sake of the hundredth person who might appreciate them, or whether the ideas for which these antiquities stood were a fundamental challenge to American conceptions." He replied, "For both reasons, but especially for the latter." He also indicated that the reason he had done all this work for the Museum of Fine Arts was essentially to make a statement against Boston's rejection of his mode of loving. "The Museum was truly a paederistic evangel," he mused in the few months left between "Johnny" Marshall's death and his own. "It must be counted a result of love."

Next time you go to a major art museum, I trust you will not just be looking at the classical art for its own sake. It's important for us also to remember that something else is here nominated in the bond, the unspoken logos of Ned Warren's challenge and humanistic vision. May it kindle our own!

Part Four:
All-American Boys

Only The Hairdresser Knew (1985)

Searching for clues in history, especially gay history, is a frustrating process. Sometimes one ends, as in the Miss Clairol ads of a few years ago, by concluding that only the hairdresser knew for sure. A serendipitous case in point occured when I was in San Francisco on a research trip in March, 1984. Here's the mystery story.

I chanced to consult some early San Francisco directories in a small research library. In front of their copy of the city directory of 1854 I found a typed note, pasted in. According to the note, on page 27 would be found an entry for the actor Edwin Booth, whose occupation was "comedian and ranchero" at the San Francisco Theater, and whose address was "rancho, Mission Road." On page 19, there would be an identical entry for David C. Anderson.

The note continued: "Edwin Booth, one of the greatest tragedians of all time, lived with David C. Anderson, his great friend, in Anderson's cottage on the Mission road, where now stands the Board of Health on Mission Street just east of 7th Street, and opposite the Post Office." The note was signed by one Luke Fay, and dated February 3, 1931.

"Great friend" is an early 20th century usage, a euphemism for "lover." Lucien Price (1883-1964), for example, uses that phrase in his gay novel sequence "All Souls," begun in 1919. So of course the tantalizing question: was the famed Shakespearean actor, brother of Lincoln's assassin John Wilkes Booth, one of us? A hundred and thirty or so years ago, Booth was an unmarried young actor who, at age 30, went out to San Francisco with his father, Junius Brutus Booth, to make some money entertaining the entrepreneurs of Baghdad-by-the-Bay and the miners whose gold was fueling the early economic development of that perennially fascinating city. The younger Booth remained behind when his father returned East, departing California only in 1856, after a long tour to Australia and the Pacific Islands. This "tryout" period, while often yielding only comic or melodramatic parts, also gave young Edwin a chance to appear in major Shakespeare roles and other classic lead parts for the first time.

Anderson was an older man, a friend of Booth's father, also an actor, and a widower. He and Booth built a two-room house in a then remote area which, because of the cheapness of housing, became a whole village of bachelor actors, called "Pipesville." Anderson and Booth listed themselves as "rancheros" and their shack as a "rancho" for a joke, of course.

It is agreed by all biographers that the two men were very strongly bonded with one another. Though eventually they went their separate ways, Booth marrying and Anderson re-marrying, it seems clear that, for Booth, later ideas of "home" were very much conditioned and shaped by the shared experience of living in this setting on the Mission Plank Road. Throughout their subsequent lives it was always to be "Davy" and "Ned" between them. Booth even supported Anderson and his second wife financially in their old age in New York City.

OK, you say, but was it a "gay" relationship in some sense? Actors are, of course, traditionally tolerant of alternate life-styles. In a two room shack, built and owned by two impecunious actors, there could only have been one bedroom and one bed. Yet, of course, in those days it was not at all unusual for two men, even total strangers, to share beds, at homes, inns, and hotels. Booth himself, in a letter to his manager in 1887, writes that on his first return trip to San Francisco, in 1876, he was approached by "every other seedy citizen" claiming that in the good old days "he used to sleep with me - as proof of our old time friendship & c... ." One would like to be able to unpack the meaning of the abbreviation for et cetera!

Gay historians, a youngish breed as historiography goes, tend to fall into two intellectual camps, the "essentialists" and the "social constructionists." The latter group focuses on the history of gay consciousness or gay identity, contending that homosexuality in our sense of the term is a recent cultural invention. To oversimplify, this means that the social meaning of homosexuality is so different in recent times that it makes no sense to talk of a homosexual identity, or of "gay people," if you will, before the modern urban-industrial period.

Where does that leave Edwin Booth? As a young man he was in San Francisco with Anderson before the ersatz term "homosexual" was manufactured. To the social constructionist, the person engaging in non-standard sexual expression was not subject then to such a labelling or stigmatizing process as would bring later gay people a sense of shame or guilt about "being different."

Martin Duberman, in *Historical Perspectives on Homosexuality*, reports on a possibly similar casual same-sex expression between two young South Carolina students. The flippancy of the two letters Duberman reprints from a collection in the South Caroliniana Library, referring to the "exquisite touches" of the other's "long fleshen pole," for example, suggests an experiential freedom which might not have been all that rare. Might it also have existed among actors in a frontier city known from the beginning for its tolerance of offbeat behavior?

Who was Luke Fay, the 1931 "labeller," and what did he know about Edwin Booth that the rest of us don't? It seems obvious to me that the note itself is a gay message, set down as some kind of signal to a future gay researcher, like a missive sealed into a bottle and cast upon the sea.

For now, all we can know is that a gay scholar in 1984 picked up a faint trace indicating that a presumably gay San Franciscan of 1931 thought, rightly or wrongly, that Edwin Booth and an actor of his father's generation had some kind of intense same-sex relationship in mid-19th century San Francisco. Was this common, or at least tolerated, in urban bohemian circles in pre-Civil War America? Certainly Walt Whitman's frequenting of Charlie Pfaff's cellar café on Broadway in New York City suggests that such "bohemian" circles were one good place to make pick-ups. And have we lost something in the way of serious but casual same-sex human relationships since the neologism "homosexual" became popular?

Was Edwin Booth gay? Maybe even his hairdresser didn't know for sure.

Swishing Through Georgia (1977)

The recent Massachusetts visit of President Jimmy Carter, late of Plains, Georgia, called up mixed memories of his fascinating home state, as well as reflections on the political and religious matrix out of which he has come. In spite of the modernity of Atlanta and the marvelous renovation of Savannah, the Civil War has faded slowly in Georgia, as any visitor can attest.

Perhaps in view of the President's visit it is appropriate to look at an earlier Georgia governor and sometime visitor to Massachusetts, albeit an involuntary one. Unlike Carter he was, if my reading of the secondary evidence is correct, a brother. This was Alexander H. Stephens, once fellow Whig Representative and friend of Abraham Lincoln, later Vice-President of the Confederacy, still later a prisoner of war in clammy Fort Warren on George's Island in Boston harbor.

Alexander Stephens was born in Wilkes County in Middle Georgia in February, 1812; his mother died about a month afterwards. The boy is described as bookish, not good at games, in delicate health, slender, and given to brooding, all of which sound suspiciously like my own early autobiography and those of many other gay youths. During his childhood his father was the center of his emotional universe, but Andrew Stephens died of pneumonia in May, 1826. The fourteen-year-old orphan then became the protegé and housemate of a 25-year-old bachelor Presbyterian minister, Alexander Hamilton Webster. We are told that young Alec (or "Ellick," as it is pronounced in Georgia) had such "prodigious" fondness for his mentor that the boy took Webster's middle name for his own. Yet Webster too died, a little over a year later, leaving the teen-aged boy desolate and abandoned once more. It is no wonder that throughout his life Stephens was given to attacks of melancholy and what his biographer, Rudolph Von Abele, calls a "consciousness of difference."

Stephens went on to teach school, read law, and get elected to Congress. In 1860 he publicly opposed secession, but like Robert E. Lee went eventually with his home state. As Vice-President of the Confederacy he was a bust, shrilly defending strict constructionist proposals against President Jefferson Davis and the realities of the wartime situation. Retiring to his home in Crawfordville, Georgia, he sat out the last part of the war. Then Stephens was captured and brought to Boston, where he was held at Ft. Warren from May 25 to October 13, 1865. Returning to his beloved "Liberty Hall" (the estate is now a Georgia state museum), he spent the next three years compiling a remarkable and virtually unreadable treatise in the form of Platonic dialogues, *A Constitutional View of the Late War Between the States*, which is chiefly devoted to demonstrating that the South had been in the right, constitutionally speaking, all along. Stephens made another, private visit to Boston in 1868 and was reelected to Congress in 1873. In 1882, elderly and almost continually ailing, he was elected Governor of Georgia, where the burden of the job killed him in less than four months.

Von Abele, writing during World War II and trying to make historical use of the psychologies of the time, described his task as "a problem in the psychology of personality, motivation, and behavior." He relies especially on "a remarkably revealing correspondence" of thirty-four years' duration between Alexander and his younger half-brother Linton, now preserved at Manhattanville College. It seems clear that Linton, who married and fathered several children, became for Alexander an object of rather more erotic feeling than brothers commonly exhibit toward one another. One might also suggest that Stephens' feelings were mixed with a desire to play the father-figure he himself had been denied.

A friend, writing of Alexander's grief after Linton's premature death, wrote "In Linton was his brother and son... . I never knew one man to love another as he loved Linton." Von Abele adds "In Linton, too, was his wife; the tenderness and passion he showed for Linton was that he had never been able to bestow on any woman." On a related level, one sees this love demonstrated in Alexander's putting between fifty and a hundred young men through college, in his commissioning a bust from a poor young sculptor and overpaying him for it, in his "fondness" at fifty for his young male secretary whom he had put through school but paid no salary until 1864, and in his law classes after the war, which brought many impoverished young men of the ruined South to the rooms of Liberty Hall.

I'm not remotely trying to say that these people were gay in any active or even dominant erotic sense, or suggesting that Liberty Hall was one vast Turkish bath or whatever. I have not read this "revealing correspondence" and for all I really know Stephens was a eunuch and Webster just a charitable Christian, and so on. I am saying that my reading of Stephens' life, coupled with my own knowledge of what it means to be gay, makes the notion of same-sex orientation at least plausible for him. And if we want to understand the workings of Eros in history it is well to remember, as Jonathan Katz reminds us in *Gay American History*, that we cannot limit ourselves to "studying only the overt or even sublimated erotic, but should take in the full range, variety, and subtlety of same-sex relations."

I'm impressed, as I've had occasion to dig into nineteenth-century primary material, with what seems to me to be a generalized homoeroticism popping up in a variety of situations from novels to college life to tramping to poetising. Certainly overt homosexual behavior was tabooed, and probably when the same-sex attachment really rose to the surface of consciousness it caused much pain (i. e., Hawthorne's rejection of Melville? Stephens' "neurasthenia"?). Yet we have constantly to deal with such suggestive bits of writing (and reading) as Bayard Taylor's supersensuous account of a (genuine) Turkish bath in *Land of the Saracens*, published at the height of a period we call "mid-Victorian."

Since Freud we have become more "sophisticated" about sex, and perhaps have less compunction about "doing it." Bringing it all to the surface has its losses, however. Probably one result has been in our century a narrowed cultural definition of what it is to be a "man," for instance. And in our pursuit of a more articulate gay consciousness we may have lost some of the freedom to accept the signals of our bodies naively, as part of the energy flow available to us by virtue of our being both animal and human.

Alexander H. Stephens as a political theorist and politician is probably of little interest to most of us. As a human being who clearly invested a lot of his energy, money and time into supportive same-sex relationships, whatever erotic component can be assigned to them, he perhaps has a greater claim to our attention, And as we proceed to seek our own "roots" by making an invisible past more visible, his life stands as a surrogate for the thousands like him in the less articulated world of antebellum America.

NOTE (1989): The latest biography, Thomas Schott's *Alexander H. Stephens of Georgia* (1988), does not address Von Abele's hypotheses concerning Stephens' erotic life, arguing instead that "it is likely that impotence was among his many physical ailments" and that "he lacked the virility of other men."

Whitman Revisited (1985)

In my younger days, gay people took their heroes and heroines from the few then known or suspected gays in history or fiction. Gay males of a literary sort had a basic choice between Oscar Wilde and Walt Whitman. Given that Whitman's birthday falls on May 31st, perhaps it is a good time to ruminate on his renewed relevance in the Age of AIDS.

As most of us are aware by now, a great deal of Whitman scholarship has gone into attempting to "prove" that he was not gay or, if the critic concedes that he leaned in that direction, to argue that these impulses are to be explained away in some elaborate symbolic fashion. This process was aided, of course, by Whitman's attempts to cover his own tracks. Although in the 1860 edition of *Leaves of Grass* he dared to publish some of his more openly homosexual love poems, he deleted the more homophilic references from later editions. School and college anthologies often reprint the final text of "Once I Passed Through a Populous City," for instance, without noting that the line "I remember only a woman I casually met there who detain'd me for love of me" is known from the original manuscript to have been "I remember only the man who wandered with me there for the love of me."

There are still many battles to be fought before the results of such seemingly arcane textual criticism get to where the average high school kid, gay or non-gay, has in his/her hands an honest rendering of what Whitman actually intended. But in these darker days, when the AIDS menace is forcing us to rethink the meaning of the elusive concept "gay community," it is also appropriate to move from the now familiar "Calamus" sequence to a renewed reading of the Civil War poems, and even more to the reworked Civil War notebooks found in the first hundred pages or so of *Specimen Days*. Those pages constitute one of the most powerful commentaries I know on the meaning of the Civil War, if not of all war.

The war experience chastened Whitman's optimism, as well as his prose style, but it did not dampen his quest to make sense of the American experience. The war erupted in 1861, soon after his "coming out" process had crystallized in the initial publication of the "Calamus" sequence. While on a visit to his wounded brother in a Virginia hospital, Walt found an appropriate, socially legitimated outlet for his homosexual impulses. Essentially he became a distinctive sort of hospital social worker. Holding down a government clerk's job by day, at night he visited the army hospitals in Washington, bearing small gifts, reciting his own poetry, dispensing such cheer as he could, reading to the boys and writing letters for them, holding them close when they needed it.

During the three years 1862-1865, Whitman estimated that he had made over six hundred visits and seen between eighty and one hundred thousand wounded and sick soldiers. He did not discriminate between white and black, Rebel or Yankee: "[I] gave them always what I had," he wrote, "and tried to cheer them the same as any." He also visited the "contraband" camps, the holding-areas for escaped slaves, "and did what I could for them."

Washington in wartime being what it was, on occasion he also picked up a healthy young soldier or other young man for the night. In his *Gay American History* Jonathan Katz has printed several germane entries from Whitman's 1862-1863 notebook: "Daniel Wilson night of Oct. 16, '62 walking up from Middagh - slept with me - works on a blacksmith shop in Navy Yard... is about 19" (Walt was 43 at the time). Or "Jerry Taylor (Oct. 9,1863; Washington) N.J of 2d dist reg't slept with me last night." Whitman also says, in *Specimen Days*, "I was among the army teamsters considerably and, indeed, found myself drawn to them." No doubt!

Back in the hospitals, though, a miracle of creative symbiosis was taking place between this middle-aged gay poet making his Quaker protest against the effects of war and these young and scared kids so far from home. Both he and they were caught up in a life-threatening scenario which could only be comprehended through the experience of being an actor within it. In those days the death rate from wounds and disease was pretty high, even assuming one made it as far as a base hospital. Small wonder that Whitman, after long hours of serving the sick and the dying, should want the comfort of a warm and living body next to him through the remainder of the night.

Whitman succeeded in establishing with these sick and dying young men a nurturing relationship, fruit of an impulse which, I think, has been underemphasized but seems to be a persistent factor in gay history, perhaps an integral part of the gay contribution. This nurturing impulse has been with us since the days of Sokrates, if not earlier. It shows up in every generation's gay priests and nuns, gay teachers, gay health workers (such as the numerous gay paramedics in Vietnam), social workers and people who elect like occupations. In the 1960's it surfaced to a marked degree in gay participation in the civil rights movement and in the revulsion over and protest against the Vietnam War. It is beginning to surface again in outrage over the Reagan administration's budget cuts in programs for the poor and uneducated and in the sanctuary and other protest movements against the not-so-covert American military operations in Central America.

I believe this life-affirming, death-denying gay nurturing impulse was present in medieval times in certain monastic orders and in those I think of as "gay saints," preeminently Francis of Assisi. And I think in the mid-1980's it is being revealed to us in a new epiphany in the work of Boston's AIDS Action Committee and similar groups in other cities, as they serve as companions and sustainers of people living with AIDS.

"Such was the war," wrote Whitman in *Specimen Days*. "It was not a quadrille in the ballroom." Neither is the AIDS fight. People are getting into that, as they did in the care of Civil War wounded, for all sorts of reasons. But in the end, it's an inner necessity, and Whitman's example still resonates. "It was in such an experience as of the war that my heart needed to be fully thrown," he wrote. "What was a man to do? The war had so much to give - there were thousands, tens of thousands, hundreds of thousands needing me - needing all who might come. What could I do?" Let us honor him by asking that question of ourselves.

All That Glitters (1985)

The period betweeen 1840 and 1890 has been described by one social historian as "the flamboyant decades of America's development." And when flamboyance reigns, can gays be far behind? The New York City material I've been uncovering in recent months while pursuing historical research suggests that we cannot.

The phrase is from Jefferson Williamson's *The American Hotel* (1930), among some pages describing the emergence of the hotel desk clerk as a new nineteenth-century occupation. The desk clerk emerges into the public conciousness about the same time as the urban luxury hotel, such as New York's Fifth Avenue Hotel (at Madison Square), said to be the first to contain a workable passenger elevator, complete with mahogany carving and plush seats.

According to Williamson, the fraternity of desk clerks shared these qualities: urbanity, superciliousness, self-regard as "a personage gifted of the gods," and either pointed mustaches or a French beard, and "no one kept it more neatly trimmed" than they. The hotel clerk was a most fashonable dresser, his shoes were polished daily and his cuffs were always immaculately white. Said one adverse critic (and these were legion), "The clerk is generally an appalling example of the extent to which dress may be carried. His shirt is always open-worked at the bosom. His waistcoat is of radiant velvet with perhaps gold buttons, and he wears diamond shirt-studs, and diamond sleeve-links that if he came by them honestly, must have cost him a couple of years' salary."

Sound gay to you? Did to me. I'm not quite sure how to unpack the phrase "if he came by them honestly." Certainly one way he came by the diamonds is that, quite often, the desk clerk was a walking display ad for the local jeweller. Given the large number of the newly rich frequenting the luxury hotels of the period, the clerk could make extra cash by referring his diamond-hungry patrons to nearby shops where diamonds could be found, or even trade in the gems himself as a sort of commission merchant to the upwardly mobile.

Desk clerking was not the only employment opportunity which brought many young men, probably disproportionately young gay men, to the rapidly expanding cities of the middle and late 19th century. Many more were clerks in the expanding office sector - Walt Whitman is an exemplar here - and salesmen or bookkeepers in the merchandising sector. Retail sales in the new dry goods "commercial palaces" offered an opportunity to dress well, meet nice people and, of course, leave one's late evenings free, all inducements for gay men then as now. (If you want confirmation of this, take a detour through the main floors of Jordan's and Filene's next time you get downtown.)

New York took the lead in the development of the modern department store, as well as in the support of specialty stores in abundance. So it did not surprise me to find reference to another bit of gay history picked up by Charles Lockwood in research for his *Manhattan Moves Uptown* (1976). *The New York Herald*, with unusual openness for the day, reported in 1846 on the case of "a young man who considers himself somewhat respectable in his community, keeping store in Warren Street," who had been arrested for his participation "in one of those revolting and disgraceful acts which are nightly practiced on the Battery or in the vicinity of City Hall." Discretion forbids description of these revolting and disgraceful acts, though I will say that if one continues to practice them nightly, one can become very proficient at them.

In any event, such young retail clerks became known in city after city as "counter-jumpers." They and their fellows congregated in rooming-houses within walking distance of the retail district, such as Beacon Hill or the South End in Boston, and presumably made friends there or at work. They may also have met, by the 1840's in New York at least, in certain bathhouses near Broadway's hotels, according to Lockwood, or in certain bars or "bohemian" hangouts. Certainly that range of turfs is familiar to most of us. I know that when I was a young man in New York in the 1950's, the Battery was said, even then, to be a nocturnal trysting-place for gay men, and for all I know it may be still.

Less amusing was the increasing prevalence of juvenile prostitution as the century wore on. Most familiar is the so-called "white slave" trade, the prostitution of young females. But there was also a fair amount of young male prostitution, ranging from outright whorehouses such as "Scotch Ann's," which flourished in the 1880's on Bleecker Street and featured young men with painted faces and women's names, to more casual, if commercial, encounters.

The famous "Cleveland Street Scandal" in London during 1889-90, involving messenger boys working for the postal telegraph system, had its American counterpart. A multi-city study of telegraph and messenger boys by the National Child Labor Committee early in this century disclosed "revelations...[which] cannot be printed or mailed, so horrifying are they," especially concerning events taking place with deliveries "after ten o'clock at night." Studies of newsboys revealed an "astounding prevalence of venereal disease," contracted in their frequent forays into "saloons, brothels and low shows in search of customers" (for their papers, that is). This brought them "into forced acquaintance with the most degraded and corrupting patrons of both sexes," according to the child labor reformer Florence Kelley, from whose essay "Child Labor and Morality" (1911) these juicy hints have come.

There is not a great deal to celebrate in reports of juvenile v.d. or of the arrest of a young clerk for seeking sexual expression in perhaps the only way open to him. The problem is, of course, that criminal and health sources leave records and personal relationships of same-sex couples, for example, most commonly do not. Yet one finds traces where one finds them, whether in the reports of civic reformers, or in pop labelling like "counter-jumper" or "Boston marriage," or even, perhaps, in the glitter palace of the supercilious desk clerk. Gay history is not all noble Grecians and mad Bavarian rulers. It is the spoor of the ordinary gay human being which most arouses the detective instinct.

NOTE (1989): In the book by Joseph Purtell, *The Tiffany Touch*, there is another instance of diamonds being a boy's best friend. Tiffany's New York diamond counter was once visited by a Texan, complete with ten-gallon hat and young man in tow complete with earrings and bracelets. They chose a $75,000 diamond ring, but said it was a bit small. The clerk, inferring the worst, told them Tiffany's did not sell men's diamond rings, but was told it was for a woman. Back in Dallas, Neiman-Marcus had no such scruples; they enlarged the ring so that it fit the young man's finger!

A Gay Academic Scandal (1977)

Last May A. Younger Gay and I left Mischief in the hands of a couple of gay friends and went South for a week's vacation. We enjoyed ourselves particularly in Williamsburg, a "first time" for A.Y.G.

Williamsburg is very straight; therefore everybody seemed to accept A. Younger Gay as my son or something without so much as looking askance. So, you are wondering, can an aging fag-of-letters find gayness in Colonial Williamsburg? Well, one evening we dropped into a local bookstore in Merchants' Square (the one with cute clerks) and discovered *The Dave Kopay Story*, Ebert's *The Homosexuals*, Simon's biography of Alice B. Toklas, and one or two more such positive gay works in this sink of right living and American traditionalism. Far out!

All during an intensive day's immersion into colonial and Revolutionary Williamsburg, I had wondered what the town had been like between 1780, when it was abandoned as the state capital, and 1926, when Colonial Williamsburg began operations. Here I found the exact book for the problem, Park Rouse Jr.'s *Cows on the Campus*, which promised (and proved) to be light but absorbing reading. And about half-way through Rouse's book, what should I encounter but you-know-what.

It seems that back in 1898, in the sleepy little college town of Willamsburg, a major scandal brewed, rocking both town and gown. Although it apparently remained an item of local gossip for many years, the first printed reference to it was in Ellen Glasgow's posthumously published autobiography, *The Woman Within* (1954), which I promptly ran down on my return.

In that spring, in search of local material for her novel *The Voice of the People*, Miss Glasgow visited Williamsburg for a month. She and her sister Cary stayed at the Colonial Inn, later razed to make room for the reconstructed Chowning's Tavern, under the grape arbor of which A. Younger and I had had a pleasant luncheon on the day I bought the Rouse book. Also living at the Inn were a number of "charming old ladies" from the First Families of Virginia, who spent their evenings retailing "more than they knew and all they suspected."

And what was there to gossip about in this quiet village in May, 1898? As Miss Glasgow charmingly put it, "the scandal was of that peculiar nature which, in the nineteenth century, before Oscar Wilde and our recent postwar fiction had made it a household word, relied entirely upon innuendo and parenthesis for distribution." The principal in the case was the Librarian of the College of William and Mary, a 35-year-old bachelor named Charles Washington Coleman, Jr., who lived with his parents in an 18th-century house still standing within the limits of the restored area.

Coleman had something of a local reputation as an essayist, poet and lecturer on literary subjects. He had attracted a small coterie of literary-intellectual students interested in such non-regulation subjects as mythology, demonology, astheticism in the arts, and the literature of the English Restoration. (Whether or not this included the Earl of Rochester's "Sodom" does not appear in the record.) Among the students was an iconoclastic and brilliant Richmond boy, James Branch Cabell, who had matriculated at age 15 and boarded during his college years at the Coleman house. Cabell, like Ellen Glasgow, was to become a significant novelist in the early years of the new century, though somewhat forgotten nowadays.

The details are murky, but here is the way it appears from the five or six germane sources I have been able to run down. There was an incident involving "student misconduct" in January, 1898, at a rowdy and alcoholic session following either a dance or (more likely) a fraternity initiation. Coleman high-tailed it out of town amidst rumors that he had been sexually involved with at least three students during that incident. The faculty, who had earlier expelled a baseball player for having "dirty words" inked on his jersey, went berserk and set up a kangaroo court, which proceeded to try "every student who had even a literary association with the supreme offender," in Miss Glasgow's words.

Faculty minutes record a discussion on March 11, 1898, from which it is clear that their investigation had zeroed in on Cabell and two other students. On April 11th, their backs evidently up, the three formally withdrew from the college, in a letter claiming that it would be "neither pleasant, nor profitable" to stay on. The same day, probably as the other half of a behind-the-scenes compromise, the faculty records indicate that "no evidence has been adduced" to justify a finding of guilty. Cabell, however, remained in Williamsburg, and there the Glasgows found him the next month.

His formidable first-family maternal parent, however, would have none of any gesture which would deprive her son of his degree and, moreover, appear to confirm his guilt. That strong-minded lady consulted with her brother-in-law, Beverly Bland Munford, a member of the College's Board of Visitors, and appeared at the Colonial Inn late in April, lawyer in tow. After a little quasi-legal negotiation with the College's President, Dr. Lyon Gardiner Tyler (son of President John Tyler), another behind-the-scenes compromise was worked out and young Cabell received his degree on schedule in June, at the ripe old age of 18.

There had been, says Glasgow (who knew Cabell extremely well in later life) "not a shred of evidence to connect James in any way with the scandal, or with the Author of Evil. There was, indeed, not anything more compromising than a shared preference for belles-lettres." All testimony, including that within his later, iconoclastic and highly sexual novels, affirms that Cabell was straight. In his own memoirs, published in 1955, he refers to his false reputation as a "pervert" and slams "catamites" who think he is one of them. Yet the rumors of this (as well as a later, equally unfounded suspicion of murder) persisted in Richmond, and Cabell still occasionally makes his way into lists of famous closeted gays.

Meanwhile, charges against Coleman were also dismissed by the faculty. I rather suspect that this too was a political move to cover the whole mess up. Of course if they had to clear all the suspected students, they had to clear Coleman, who couldn't have committed sodomy with himself. (Well, it isn't likely that he would have done it at a fraternity initiation, in 1898 at least.)

Coleman found it expedient to resign from William and Mary anyway, citing the need for extensive medical treatment for arm injuries received in a fall from a library ladder. (Dangerous places, libraries.) Moving to

Washington, D. C., he secured a position on the staff of the Library of Congress, becoming head of circulation there in 1909. Of his other Williamsburg experiences, we have record that at least the writing of essays and poetry continued. He also made it into *Who's Who in America*, which after a certain age is a substitute for other kinds of satisfactions.

From thence he disappears from the record, however; missing and presumed dead by the editors of *Who Was Who in America*, who concluded in 1968 that anyone they could not track down born more than a century earlier was more than likely six feet under. (If Coleman were alive, he'd be 115 years old now.) He is said never to have recovered from the ordeal of 1898. But one has the lingering hope that he found some consoling experiences and went out with panache, like the poet of Antiquity who died at the age of eighty locked in the embrace of a handsome young boy. (Anyway, aren't gay librarians supposed, in Oscar Wilde's famous phrase, to begin each morning at the bottom of a new page?)

The Williamsburg scandal of 1898 resonates 79 years later, when the issue of the rights of gays to exist as teachers and other "role models" for the young is once again being called into vociferous question. It is probable in 1898 that the Oscar Wilde trial and conviction two years earlier, given an upper and upper middle class interest in all things British in the 1890's, had brought at least elliptical discussion and therefore stimulated suspicion of homosexuality in quarters in America where it would not have been earlier considered an acceptable topic of conversation. Now, since Anita Bryant & Co. have once again made the welkin ring with their sticky charges of child molestation, I think it reasonable to expect that school boards and vigilante committees, even here, will be looking more closely into the personal lives of their unmarried teachers.

Renewed emphasis on the slippery term "role model" stacks the deck with a wild card, and there is irony in the fact that it was originally provided by gay rhetoricians. The milder homophobes will argue, I suspect, that it is not a matter of being against either homosexual orientation or freedom of expression; they just want "positive role models" (the new code words for straight) in the classroom. "Role model" in this context will, wherever possible, be used to distract attention from actual performance. Coleman had, after all, considerable ability to engage students in intellectual concerns and in that sense was a very positive role model. But Sokrates did the same thing, and look what happened to him.

We need to look to the dryness of our powder and the penetrating power of our shot. For when what Miss Glasgow called "the mob spirit, carefully veiled, had awakened in the minds of the best people" in Williamsburg in

1898, Branch Cabell, straight though he may have been, and Charles Coleman, gay though he may have been, found no defenders, "Sheep are not the only creatures that run together," comments Miss Glasgow. Amen to that.

A Forgotten Gay Novelist (1977)

The recent announcement by a New York City reprint house that it is republishing the collected works of Henry Blake Fuller has not exactly sent shock waves through the gay community. Henry Blake Fuller? Who's he?

A Chicagoan derived from the same New England family which whelped Margaret and R. Buckminster Fuller, Henry Fuller wrote a number of realistic and romantic novels in the 1890's, the best of them *With The Procession*, a novel of Chicago society. He was later associated with Harriet Monroe on *Poetry* magazine, and was always open to new currents in American writing. In 1918, past his sixtieth birthday, he completed *Bertram Cope's Year*, which probably stands as the first unambiguously gay American novel by a respected novelist.

Fuller had this work issued in 1919 through a friend's small publishing house and paid for the cost of publication, after several larger firms had rejected it. Friends and the literary public either ignored, misunderstood, or severely criticized it. Fuller's reaction was to destroy the manuscript, the proofs, and all unsold copies (about two-thirds of the small printing). The depth of his pain is indicated by the fact that, although he continued to write literary criticism in the 1920's for national journals, he did not attempt another novel for ten years.

Fuller, like others of his family, was a creative eccentric. He was a very private (read "discreet"?) person who lived in a succession of cheap rooming-houses at the edges of the University of Chicago community. The internal evidence of his work (which is demonstrably autobiographical in other respects), relevant sections of his youthful journals (at 19, he writes "I would pass by twenty beautiful women to look upon a handsome man") and scattered other pieces of evidence all warrant the conclusion that he was gay, though perhaps not sexually active, even abroad. (He did make several trips to Italy, however, and after reading Roger Peyrefitte's *The Exile of Capri* I now suspect everyone who travelled to Italy in the 1890's.)

Some may find such evidence in his first short story, which centered on a Venetian gondolier. After all, wasn't it in Venice that the authorities once ordered prostitutes to stand in their windows with breasts bared, in an unsuccessful attempt to attract Venetian men away from the youths they were all too openly attracted to? But Fuller's first explicit attempt at a literary "coming out" was a play, "At St. Jude's," available in a volume of short plays in the style of Maeterlinck called *The Puppet-Booth* (1896) and published when Fuller was 39 years old. "At St Jude's" is an unactable, unsuccessful melodrama taking place in the sacristy of a church, where a young bridegroom is found waiting for his bride. His roommate and best friend tries to talk him out of it, claiming he has loved the other man all his life and will not permit the marriage. Eventually the groom has to kill his best friend in order to enter the church. (Not Fuller's best plot!)

Four years later, in *The Last Refuge*, Fuller depicted a middle-aged bachelor-dreamer (clearly the author himself) who makes another pilgrimage to Italy in the company of a beloved but self-centered (and, in the event, straight) young man. Fuller did have a genuine gift for relating to and encouraging younger men, including young writers of the 1920's, and he was to repeat in actuality the protagonist's role in his final trip to Italy in 1924. The theme of an older man trying to find a sympatico younger male to travel or live with him recurs frequently in Fuller's writings; those who have been through the experience will no doubt take this as a further sign of his gayness.

With *Bertram Cope's Year*, however, Fuller really came out of the literary closet. Copies of the original edition are exceedingly scarce. My memories of it are from reading it in the University of Chicago library fifteen years ago; I was unable to locate copies either at Boston Public (which has several Fuller works) or any other library immediately accessible to me.

Let it suffice to say here that most of the straight critics, either in the 'twenties or in the current modest revival of interest in Fuller, have not known how to deal with it. One literary scholar, in a book published only five or six years ago, thinks it "unsuccessful" because of Fuller's "failure to deal adequately with the impact of sexual aberration upon the lives of his characters. Although he supplied abundant evidence of the homosexual tendencies of all the major male characters," writes this critic, "he never once indicated the tension or emotional conflicts which accompany or result from their sexual deviations." (I should say that this benighted soul teaches at the University of Mississippi, which clearly cannot any longer be thought of as the fag end of creation!)

The reliably perceptive Edmund Wilson, however, in an important essay in the May 23, 1970 *New Yorker* (conveniently reprinted in his posthumous *The Devil and Canon Barham*), calls Fuller "a unique and distinguished writer." Deploring its lack of serious attention from students of literature, Wilson terms *Bertram Cope's Year* "perhaps Fuller's best" book. Wilson sees the work as rising to a level beyond its realistic, Howells-type novelistic counterparts. And he argues that it is not really about homosexuality per se, but rather about the effects of sexual magnetism in general, in which Fuller "merely... extended what was then the conventional range."

Ah, yes, but to extend the conventional range in 1918 was not to do it "merely." This was, after all, before Gide was widely known in this county and before Proust had been translated. *Bertram Cope's Year*, as I recall it, is very matter-of-fact about homosexuality. The state is neither perverse nor shameful, its fictional treatment neither pornographic nor propagandistic. At the end there is neither happiness nor tragedy. The self-centered Cope simply picks up his master's degree and goes off to another city to take a teaching position. It is left uncertain to a wealthy middle aged woman and an aging gay male friend (both of whom had wishful thoughts about Cope) as to whether our non-hero will take up with the young lady with whom he has been corresponding or the effeminate young man with whom he has been rooming.

In 1918 Fuller was taking for granted (as is evidenced both in the content of the book and the author's extreme shock at its reception) what Evelyn Hooker began to confirm scientifically in the 1950's. His hidden argument is, briefly, that homosexuality is a variation within the normal range, and it's time we really accepted it as such and went on from there. I've read a number of "liberated" gay novels in the past few years and, with all due respect, few of them impress me as having more than a transient propaganda value. It may be that reissue of the works of an accomplished stylist who has earned a worthy place in American letters will stimulate contemporary gay novelists and playwrights to a greater sense of the importance of form and craftsmanship, as well as to a more finely honed awareness of the power of persuasion by indirection.

There, now! Isn't that more than you ever wanted to know about Henry Blake Fuller?

NOTE (1989): The announcement of a Fuller reprint series was evidently another standard reprint house ploy to test the market for advance orders before going ahead with the project; the announced collection appears never to have been published. A reprint of *Bertram Cope's Year* is, however, listed in the current *Books in Print* as an item in AMS Press' "Gay

Experience" series. I should also say, given my rather cutting remark about contemporary gay novels, that the years since 1977 have seen an extraordinary flowering of significant novels by the likes of Andrew Holleran, Paul Monette, Robert Ferro, Edmund White, David Leavitt and others too numerous to mention.

Public (and Private) Affairs (1984)

In his last letter to Thomas Jefferson, that stout old Federalist John Adams commented that "Public affairs go on pretty much as usual; perpetual chicanery and rather more personal abuse than there used to be." As the current election season creeps and crawls toward its miserable conclusion, one appreciates the sprightly wisdom of the nonagenarian ex-President as a rare shaft of honest light in a prospect of increasing intellectual darkness.

There are few grounds for optimism on the current political landscape, but surely one of them is the increased electoral visibility of gay and lesbian voters, action groups, and candidates. The day before the Massachusetts primary, for example, my mail contained a packet of materials from the Massachusetts Gay Political Caucus, including a record of how each state legislator voted on the last gay rights bill. It also contained endorsements of pro-gay candidates for Congress and the state legislature who "expressed a desire to be included" in such a list to such an audience. Remarkably, nearly forty Massachusetts politicians requested such a listing.

The first openly gay politician to seek municipal office in the U.S. was the San Francisco transvestite entertainer José Sarria, who ran for City Supervisor in 1961 and polled an astonishing 7000 voters city-wide. It took district election systems, however, to permit the election of openly gay persons to the governing boards of San Francisco (Harvey Milk, 1977) and Boston (David Scondras, 1983). Elaine Noble, also of Boston, was the first open lesbian to be elected to a state legislature (1974). This year Massachusetts once again leads the procession with the first decloseted, self-affirming gay member of Congress likely to win re-election to the House of Representatives, Gerry Studds.

Of course Studds is hardly the first gay man to serve in the Congress. William "Fishbait" Miller, an employee of the House for forty-two years, describes a few in his 1977 memoirs. One congressman was picked up by police in rural Virginia under ambiguous circumstances involving a boy in his automobile. Capital Hill gossips averred that the case was never prosecuted because the lawmaker had swallowed the evidence. Certain legislators were also rumored to hire male staffers in part for their willingness to engage in sex. The latter were known as "hill monkeys," since they held on to their jobs "by the tail."

Then there was U.S. Senator David Ignatius Walsh of Massachusetts, gay as the proverbial goose. (Why geese should be gayer than, say, monkeys has never been self-evident.) Walsh was a poor Irish kid from northern Worcester County who was graduated from the College of the Holy Cross and rose to become Massachusetts' first governor and U.S. Senator of Irish Catholic ancestry.

"Fishbait" Miller relays a Walsh story I'd never heard. It seems that a leading department store owner (Edward Filene?) once remarked that he'd be happy to entrust his daughter to Walsh even if he proposed to take her across the Atlantic on a yacht. But, according to Miller, "he wouldn't trust his son to the Senator's benign care across the Charles River in a canoe." (Dangerous places, canoes!)

In his *The Homosexual Matrix* (1975), C. A. Tripp tells an interesting story about Sen. Walsh. During World War II Walsh chaired the Senate Committee on Naval Affairs, certainly an appropriate committee, in that he had a good bit of experience in such affairs. On Pacific Street in Brooklyn, near the Brooklyn Navy Yard, there was a thriving male bordello which specialized in introductions to servicemen. In addition to serving up sea food to a variety of clients, the house also attracted foreign espionage agents, who plied the willing sailors and their customers with drink while attempting to pick up secret information concerning ship movements.

An ideal spot for a raid, one would think, as did Naval Intelligence once they got wind of it. But a couple of funny things happened on their way to Pacific Street. For one thing, according to the proprietor's sworn testimony (corroborated by several sailors), they discovered that the chairman of the Senate Committee on Naval Affairs was a house "regular." For another, Sen. Walsh had not been seen on Pacific Street since just the day before the Navy began full-time surveillance from a hospital room opposite the building. Of course as chairman of Naval Affairs, Walsh was regularly briefed on proposed Naval Intelligence operations, especially sensitive ones like this.

Somehow the word got out that a highly placed member of Congress had been implicated in the raid. But the government, looking for a formula which would protect one of the Senate's most powerful members, did not act. *The New York Post* printed as much as it dared, while the gay members of Congress shook in their shoes. Walsh went about his official business, denying that he had ever stayed overnight in any house in Brooklyn, which may well have been true. J. Edgar Hoover and the F. B. I. were brought into it to prepare a report protecting Sen. Walsh, undoubtedly on orders from the White House. There were official and public denials that Sen. Walsh had ever gone to a house of depravity in Brooklyn in order to meet German spies. Few noticed that the statement was carefully constructed to slip around acknowledging any possibility that he may have gone to such a place for some equally subversive, though less political, purpose.

A few years after Walsh's death there appeared a biography by Dorothy Wayman, published by the Catholic publishing house of Bruce in Milwaukee. Wayman denied that the Senator, whose practicing Catholicism she stresses, could ever have patronized the "loathsome dive" on Pacific Street, declining to repeat the "unprintable details of perversion and degradation" which had been bruited about concerning it. Ms. Wayman then reprints J. Edgar Hoover's letter giving Walsh a clean bill of health, and goes on to praise the F.B.I.'s investigators as "America's finest body of highly trained, deeply loyal and assiduously active investigators of subversion and illegal activities," presumably including homosexuality. She sees the whole episode as one fabricated in an attempt to advance "the subversive ends of those who hated America." So much for perpetual chicanery.

For many years now the Charles River Esplanade has been a post-midnight resort for Boston gay men seeking sexual adventure. Among the bronze statues of Massachusetts worthies overlooking that hallowed ground is - you guessed it - one of U.S. Senator David Ignatius Walsh. Or hadn't you noticed?

NOTE (1989): Since this essay was published, a second gay member of Congress from Massachusetts, Barney Frank, has "come out" publicly and, like Studds, has been re-elected afterwards. Robert Parker's *Capitol Hill in Black and White* (1986) has some further anecdotal material on gay U.S. Senators.

Part Five:
Sex in the Sacristy

Sex and the Single Priest (1981)

"Palimony" is in the news again, and wouldn't you know that this time it involves a gay Episcopalian! According to everybody's favorite bathroom reading, the *National Enquirer*, John Michael Tebelak, creator of "Godspell," is being sued for half the royalties of that remarkable theatre piece by one Richard Hannum, identified as the homosexual lover with whom Tebelak shared seven years of companionship. The attorney for the plaintiff, Marvin Mitchelson, has taken that role in other highly publicized cases of this sort dating back to the "palimony" lawsuit of Lee Marvin and Michelle Triola.

The *National Enquirer* is not, of course, an entirely credible source. My local diocesan newspaper indicates the further fact that Tebelak is now a candidate for Holy Orders in the Diocese of New York. Well, good for Tebelak, and I hope he makes it through; the church needs his kind of creative talent. But is the Episcopal church ready for a gay priest who will have been through the ordeal of massive national publicity concerning his sex life, should this case come to trial? Especially one who, in *Enquirer*-cited direct quotes, admits to simultaneous involvements with other men while living with Hannum? Stay tuned, folks... .

To be sure, the Episcopal church (not to mention others) has always ordained gay clergy and, for that matter, consecrated gay bishops. One of the many differences between now and the bygone era in which I was a boy soprano is that then nobody ever talked about it. Many, if not most, of these gay priests lived out their lives serving God in their generation and parish. A few got caught out at some sexual indiscretion and were forced to leave off practicing their ministry. We hear more, of course, of the latter group. Hastings Rashdall once wrote apropos of the medieval university that "the life of the virtuous student has no annals," and probably one can say much the same thing of virtuous priests.

This past year I have set myself a course of readings in the history of the American Episcopal church. One of several books passing under my eye has been Bruce Steiner's biography of Bishop Samuel Seabury. On page 72 of that absorbing volume appears an account of how young Mr. Seabury's clerical fortunes were advanced when the rectorship of St. Peter's, Westchester was fortuitously opened before him in 1765. It appears that Seabury's immediate predecessor in that church, a hard-working young Princeton graduate named John Milner, had involuntarily concluded an otherwise highly successful ministry of four years in Westchester after allegations that, while intoxicated, he had molested the son of one of his churchwardens.

Milner himself never confessed to this indiscretion and, says Steiner, "there was some reason, though not much, to doubt the truth of the story." Without waiting around for a formal hearing, however, Milner decamped to Virginia, where he was promptly made Rector of Newport parish, Isle of Wight County. News of this appointment, of course, merely confirmed opinions held by Episcopalians of impeccable morals and Northeastern residence concerning the laxity of the Church of England in Virginia.

Hoping to discover more concerning the fortunes of this hapless cleric, I turned to James McLaughlin's biographical directory of early Princetonians. It appears that Milner (Class of 1758) was ordained in 1761 by the bishop of London, and was only 27 years young at the time he high-tailed it out of St. Peter's, claiming that an unspecified enemy in the parish had made it impossible for him to vindicate himself. Five years later, however, his new vestry also forced his resignation "to escape trial on charges of immoral conduct," nature unspecified. Thence, at age 32, Milner virtually disappears from the public record; McLaughlin was unable to discover where or when he died or where his gay bones lie.

Scanning the remaining biographies to find out if I could discover any more gay Princetonians, I had but little success. One John Wright, Class of 1752, had been described by none other than Jonathan Edwards as "a person of very good character for his understanding, prudence, and piety." Wright became a very effective New Light Presbyterian preacher in western Virginia, but appears to have sunk into some form of mental illness late in 1757. In 1759 the Hanover Presbytery found him guilty of drunkenness. In 1761 Wright was the central figure at a church trial, called because another clergyman had accused him of "the horrid Crime of Sodomy" as well as "Drunkenness, Popery and Racing," in that order. His accuser later apologized for repeating mere hearsay. But two years later the Presbytery suspended Wright, for reasons unspecified in the published account, and he too then disappears from the record.

Were these two men the earliest gay clergy in America? Probably not. It may be possible to track others, since this was a day when clergy even more than now acted as moral policemen against their erring brethren. There are probably, therefore, other manuscript records as yet unexamined, references buried in clerical diaries or correspondence, or reports to the Society for the Propagation of the Gospel. Where is the gay church historian who will dig them out for us?

Let me close with two other tidbits from the annals of gay Anglicanism, both found in the respected British historian Hugh Trevor-Roper's "King James and his Bishops" (*History Today*, Vol. 5, 1955). I refer specifically to Trevor-Roper's accounts of two Archbishops of Canterbury, the Jacobean incumbent George Abbot and the future incumbent William Laud, now honored in some quarters (including the *Lesser Feasts and Fasts*) as a martyr of the church. It is, of course, well known that James I, the learned Head of the Church at the time of the initial settlement of these American colonies, was as gay as the proverbial goose, most flagrantly so as the lover of George Villiers, Duke of Buckingham ("Christ had his John, and I have my George").

What I had not previously known is that this celebrated tete à tete was brought about by none other than George, Archbishop of Canterbury. "A skilful courtier," says Trevor-Roper, [Abbott] "realized that the best way in which the Archbishop of Canterbury could keep in with the Head of the Church was by inserting a personable young man into the royal bedchamber; and it was he who thus introduced George Villiers into that important apartment." A rival court faction, we are told, "found another young Adonis, washed his face every morning with posset-curds, and thrust him under the King's eye," but to no avail.

Within a decade Buckingham was in actual control of appointments to Church of England bishoprics, and one way or another his attentions were being cultivated by every rising cleric. Hence these entries in Laud's diaries: "Tonight I could dream of nothing but the Duke of Buckingham...." and "I dreamed that the Duke of Buckingham came into bed with me and showed me great affection."

Gay clergypersons, some advice. Keep no diaries!

NOTE (1989): John Michael Tebelak died of heart failure on April 2, 1985, age 36. At the time of his death he was Dramaturge of the Cathedral of St. John the Divine, whose new theatre was appropriately named in his memory.

A Tale of Four Churches (1980)

As I write, a crow calls in the distance. A red squirrel, chattering indignantly at my cat Mischief, makes its way through the pines alongside the sunny balcony where I sit. The sky is that peculiar shade of azure which is the wonder and despair of Provincetown artists. The air is fresh, the sun mellow. It is North Truro, on Cape Cod, early on an August morning.

In the past few days I have visited four churches, two of them nineteenth century white clapboarded Congregational meeting houses, and two twentieth century Episcopal structures. The oldest is the meeting house in Truro Center, where I attended a viola concert benefitting the restoration of the bell tower. The Revere bell rang right merrily for us, straight and gay alike, to summon us in from the warm night. The congregation was organized as a church in 1709, the same year as the town government. But by 1827 the center of population had moved from North Truro to Truro Center, and it was decided to build a new and more convenient meetinghouse, high on the hill next to the town's windmill. The stated reasons for the location were "to serve as a beacon for sailors, and to be closer to God."

Nowadays the congregation is so small it cannot sustain a year-round minister, and services are held in the old meetinghouse only in the summer months. But in 1827 the need both for God and for a beacon was a constant in this seafaring community. One walks through the churchyard, coming upon gravestones in memory of young men "lost at sea." One large marble monument carries the names of 57 "citizens of Truro," mostly in their teens and twenties, two of them twelve years of age, the crews of seven ships lost in a single storm in October, 1841. This quiet country graveyard conveys a real sense of the "otherness" of the past, of lives played out in a setting dependent on the bounty of the sea, but often enough reaping a harvest of its terrors as well.

The second church is that of Wellfleet, originally the village and parish of Billingsgate, and the town just south of Truro. In contrast to the very plain Truro Center meeting house, the 1850 Wellfleet structure has a pilastered and pedimented and corniced Greek revival front and a templed bell-tower. Remodelling the building in 1873 to add an organ niche and stained glass windows (so the congregation could sleep in a subdued light, as the old joke has it), the then wealthy congregation turned to the Boston organ-builders Hook and Hastings for a new tracker organ complete with high Victorian black walnut case.

Fortunately for us, the late nineteenth century decline of Wellfleet's population and of its wealth from fishing, followed by the twentieth century decline in church membership, meant that the congregation could never afterward afford a new organ. Now that we are beginning to appreciate the craftsmanship of the late nineteenth century American organ builders, instruments like this one are being revalued and restored. I was there for another benefit recital, along with a lot of elderly couples and a handful for other gays. (Organ recitals seem to bring us out of the woodwork, if not out of the closet.) And, except for an ill-advised attempt on the part of the organist to demonstrate that both he and the instrument could handle some really big-bang-Bach/Vivaldi (unsuccessful on both counts), it was a rich experience. The Hook and Hastings firm produced organs in that period equal to the best abroad; if you've never heard Franck and other French romantics on such a period instrument, you have been truly deprived.

My third church is the (Episcopal) St. Mary of the Harbor in Provincetown, that sink of iniquity conveniently located just northwest of where I summer in North Truro. The building is "made over" from an old salt house (the nave) and a fisherman's clubhouse (the chancel). Some early members of the congregation were prominent artists; one designed the new church (dedicated in 1936) and others have given of their talents to fashion paintings and sculpture for the little church and its lovely lich-gated garden.

The sea is close here too; in fact, it laps against the seawall just behind the chancel. After the benediction each Sunday the congregation, still kneeling, sings "Eternal Father, Strong to Save" in continuing remembrance of "those in peril on the sea." In the Epiphany mural over the altar, figures representing the fishermen and the artists of Provincetown come together in contemplation of the symbol of the Trinity. The simplicity of the church, its proportions, and sheer appropriateness of its assemblage of church art all give new meaning to the phrase "the beauty of holiness."

Gays are there too, of course, both local and visitors. Many of the local straights are fairly elderly and pretty low-church; in fact, one way you tell the gays from the straights is to see who's genuflecting at appropriate moments. As a regular communicant of a parish church so high that newcomers are well advised to bring anti-vertigo pills to the major feasts, I am somewhat bemused by all this, but I restore my equilibrium by surreptitiously making sheep's eyes at a blond hunk in the choir.

My last church is the summer chapel of St. James the Fisherman in Wellfleet, whose congregation began meeting just thirty summers ago. This 1957 structure, set on a hill covered with pines, was designed by a Scandinavian architect once associated with the Saarinens, and in it the congregation surrounds the altar. Its symbol, the scallop shell, represents both St. James and the Town seal of Wellfleet. Its interior might have been designed by a nineteenth century shipwright, and its bell tower shares with Truro's and St. Mary's the shape and character of a beacon.

The founding priest of St. James was the late Bishop James A. Pike, then Chaplain of Columbia University and later Dean of the Cathedral Church of St. John the Divine, who summered in Wellfleet during the 1950's. The land was given by a retired professor in my university; his ashes and those of his wife lie buried beside the chapel. Their daughter, who had been on the building committee, invited me over a few days ago for a late-afternoon drink in her garden, and we reminisced about the James Pike we had known in the 1950's. He had told her that he regarded the building of St. James' Chapel as one of the high points of his ministry. And when I asked if there was any special memorial to him in the chapel, she replied that the chapel itself was his memorial. "St. James the Fisherman" - yes, indeed an appropriate remembrance.

He had, don't you know, a gay son. The story, told in William Stringfellow and Anthony Townes' *The Death and Life of Bishop Pike*, is painful to read. James Pike was not comfortable with the homosexual orientation, though he tried to understand it. His son Jim Jr. felt degraded by the discovery of homosexuality in himself, could get no help or keys to self-affirmation from the other homosexuals he encountered, and took his own life in February, 1966 (the same year his father was censured by the House of Bishops) by putting a rifle bullet through his brain in a run-down hotel near the Everard Baths in New York City.

I remember reading a newspaper account of Jim Jr.'s death, and saying to myself "It's because he's a homosexual," though I had no independent evidence for it. Somehow in those days when there was a suicide and the papers said there was no apparent reason for it, you could just know, and know also it might have been you. Since I've read *The Death and Life of Bishop Pike* I can't pass the tower of St. James the Fisherman, high above Route 6, without thinking of the two James Pikes, each in his own way a martyr to the odium theologicum. And I wonder whether it is Jim Sr.'s heresy of the mind or Jim Jr.'s heresy of the body which is the more threatening to the present-day leaders of the Episcopal Church.

Four churches, four sacred spaces, four occasions for prayer and reflection. Nature is here, and God, and caring and creative men and women who, in these specific places on the Lower Cape, have responded to the presence of God in Christ and in each other.

Remembering the two James Pikes, and all those saints and martyrs who have gone before us, let us draw strength from the grace of God and the presence of the Holy Spirit in our midst. Let us resolve anew to share our strengths with our sisters and brothers in peril on the restless waves of ignorance and prejudice. Like the meetinghouse at Truro, let us serve as a beacon for these storm-tossed sailors, and so let us learn to be closer to God.

NOTE (1989): In 1985, the conservative southern Presiding Bishop of the Episcopal Church retired and was replaced by Edmund Browning, who as Bishop of Hawaii had strongly supported lesbians and gay men in and out of the church. In his first address following his selection as Presiding Bishop and Primate, Bishop Browning proclaimed that "this church of ours is open to all; there will be no outcasts...." Since then, while older ways of dividing off groups still exist within the Episcopal church, they are no longer sanctioned at the top.

A Memorable Gay Hoax (1980)

On one of last summer's pleasanter days I was browsing through a book sale in the courtyard of the Boston Public Library when a lavender and magenta dust jacket caught my eye. It proved to contain W. A. Swanberg's *The Rector and the Rogue* (1968), described as "being the TRUE & INCREDIBLE Acc't of a DASTARDLY HOAX against an Upright (if rather stuffy) Divine. It turned N.Y. *upside down* ."

Never one to pass by amusing books about nineteenth century America, New York City, or the foibles of my fellow Episcopalians, I leapt upon it and headed home to savor the contents. As I read, the feeling grew upon me that this affair had a subtly gay ambience, and so indeed it proved. Since this spring of 1980 marks its centennial, let me call to our collective memory what seems to have been the greatest, most elaborate, most high-church-camp-style hoax ever perpetrated on these shores.

I once heard the late Bishop (then merely Dean) James A. Pike opine concerning Episcopalians that "many are cold, but few are frozen." The Rev. Morgan Dix, S.T.D., fifty-two-year-old Rector of Trinity Parish in February, 1880 (and for twenty-eight years thereafter) was unquestionably one of the frozen few. Chief minister since 1852 of one of New York's oldest, and certainly its wealthiest and most prestigious religious foundation, Dr. Dix had championed the newer, more ritualistic tendencies within the American Episcopal church. In 1874 he had thawed sufficiently to wed a charming young lady twenty-three years his junior, and moved uptown to a new Rectory next to Trinity Chapel, off fashionable Madison Square.

Much to the Rector's surprise and subsequent dismay, on Wednesday, Feb. 18, 1880 a salesman showed up to sell him an office safe, followed by a teacher from St. John's School for Girls seeking to enroll his then infant daughter. Next came a hostler leading a pair of bay horses, a toupée maker, and the representative of a dancing school, all bearing postcards requesting their presence and (allegedly) signed by the Rector. For the next three days the procession increased, including four salesmen for church organs and three for farm equipment, plus dozens of pieces of mail with free samples and advertisements for various oddly assorted pieces of merchandise.

Sunday was a day of respite, but on Monday morning a series of twenty-eight old-clothes dealers began showing up at regular intervals, followed by fifteen pawnbrokers and by several eminent physicians who had been hastily summoned to Dr. Dix's supposed deathbed. The next morning a series of shoe dealers arrived, followed by fourteen clergymen bearing fake invitations to lunch with a visiting English bishop. In the course of the afternoon Dix was visited by an angry husband with whose wife the harassed Rector was said to have arranged a rendezvous. I refer you to Swanberg's book for elaboration, and simply say that over the course of the hoax over 500 people were invited to the Rectory, including a tattoo artist, several undertakers, and four lawyers who called to assist the pregnant Mrs. Dix in securing a divorce.

A similar hoax, on which this one was later shown to have been modelled, had been arranged by one Theodore Hook in London in 1810. But this one in some respects out-did Hook and certainly eclipsed all other American practical jokesters, baffling Dr. Dix and the police and postal inspectors for weeks. The initial clues were two letters, one to Dix signed "Gentleman Joe," asking a fee of $1000 to get the thing stopped, and one in the *New York Times* signed "High Churchman," clearly from the same person. Then a New York broker who had read press accounts (which broke only on March 13th) recalled a similar though smaller-scaled caper he had encountered while in London some seven years earlier.

The perpetrator of that prank was one E. Fairfax Williamson, a luxury-loving American dilettante who claimed kinship with the Fairfaxes of Virginia. This reddish-brown-bearded "glass of fashion and mold of form" had organized the hoax as revenge against an ex-landlord, had been caught, and had been sentenced to a year in Pentonville, a prison later to be graced by the blubbering presence of Oscar Wilde. Williamson had told several people at the time that he had once taught Sunday School in Trinity Chapel.

Williamson, when tracked down in Baltimore by the postal inspectors, proved to be the eccentric, practical joke-loving scion of a Pittsburgh family, an afficionado of French and Italian figurines and of German and Swiss music boxes, and a collector of autographed pictures of Episcopal bishops and other celebrities. Through his membership in Pittsburgh's wealthy (and very High) St. Andrew's Episcopal Church, he had come to know the Carnegies and other magnates, and used the fashionable Anglo-Catholic churches here and abroad to gain access to other wealthy families. From all accounts, he was a personable and charming fellow.

Williamson was especially fond of children, frequently taking them to museums, concerts, and circuses, and occasionally giving them elaborate gifts, such as a diamond pin to the son of a leading Pittsburgh financier and a gold watch to the son of a contractor. Rather more to the point, Fairfax had taught Sunday School at Trinity Chapel from 1869 to 1871, while falsely posing as a Wall Street broker. He had been dismissed by Dix, however, for what the Victorians called "improper conduct" with one or more boys in the junior choir.

In March, 1880 Fairfax was booked on charges of forgery and attempted extortion and sent to the Tombs, New York's fearsome detention center for those awaiting trial. Upon entrance he was recognized by the Warden as one who, five years earlier, had been his temporary guest following charges of molestation brought by a Western Union telegraph boy with a penchant for blackmail. According to the *New York Times,* Williamson had gone to Dr. Dix for bail money, had been (predictably) refused, had raised bail elsewhere, and then had left town without waiting for the formality of a trial.

Any hopes Williamson might have had of having his hoax to be taken as a bad practical joke or a sign of mild insanity were queered (as it were) by the revelation of his homosexuality. Dr. Dix himself gave the newspapers the story about the dismissal for a reason "so horrible that I don't like to tell it;" after that, he didn't need to do so. Nor did it help matters that Williamson had been a Confederate agent during the Late Unpleasantness Between the States; the judge was a former Union Army officer who had marched with Sherman through Georgia. "Gentleman Joe" was sentenced to three and one half years at hard labor, developed a severe case of stomach ulcers while in prison, and died on December 22, 1880, after less than eight months in Sing Sing.

Down on lower Broadway, opposite Wall Street, still stands Trinity Church, once the tallest structure in the city, now dwarfed by the temples of Mammon. Inside, the curious traveller will find the Chapel of All Saints, built in memory of Dr. Dix, his venerated bones under the altar, and his recumbent effigy on a cenotaph of marble, geologically symbolic of his image in life. Up on West Twenty-fifth Street Richard Upjohn's brownstone Trinity Chapel (now the Serbian Orthodox Cathedral of St. Saba) and

Clergy House still survive, as does the fanciful Trinity Chapel School building in Ruskinian polychrome, an appropriate setting for the Sunday School classes once taught by the polychromatic E. Fairfax Williamson.

An organization called the "Gay American Historical Society" (of which I should like to know more) has recently placed a historical tablet on the Stonewall Inn building on Christopher Street. If marking gay historic sites becomes a habit, may I suggest one of these church buildings for a marker in memory of a man whom Swanberg calls "this king [queen?] of practical jokers" and "a great and neglected American," our gay brother E. Fairfax Williamson, alias "Gentleman Joe," "High Churchman," "The Duke of Sing Sing," and whatever else? The Rev. Dr. Morgan Dix has been amply memorialized by an upright (if rather stuffy) heterosexual Anglican posterity. Is it not proper for us partially to turn N.Y. *upside down* once more and redress the balance for one of our own?

Gregory's Angels and All That (1981)

Paddy Kitchen's excellent brief biography of our brother Gerard Manly Hopkins, priest and poet, was written for the best of reasons. "Hopkins is my favorite poet," says the author, "and I was curious to explore the creative chemistry behind the words that affect me, an agnostic, so strongly."

As Ms. Kitchen shows, one catalyst in this "creative chemistry" was what the dust jacket describes as "his involuntary attraction to handsome boys," an attraction Hopkins attempts to sublimate in some of his poetry. It is neither the first nor the last time that such impulses have been the wellsprings of artistic creation, and how nice it is that the biographers are now willing to trace these connections publicly.

Nowhere in Hopkins' poetry is the link stronger, and the dilemmas of dealing with fleshly passions more directly addressed, than in "To what serves Mortal Beauty?" Physical beauty is "dangerous" for the celibate priest, yet Hopkins must acknowledge that it "does set dancing blood." And what model does Hopkins call on to solve such a problem? Not Heloise and Abelard, you may be sure. Rather it is Pope Gregory the Great (d. 604), saint in the Roman and Anglican calendars (Feast Day March 12th).

Gregory was a patrician, a founder of monasteries, a diplomat, an innovator. Says the *Lesser Feasts and Fasts*, "his ordering of the Church's liturgy and chant has molded the spirituality of the Western Church until the present day." The Venerable Bede refers to him as "our own apostle," for it was Gregory who, in 596, sent a group of his own monks to Britain, led by the future St. Augustine of Canterbury. In 601 Augustine was given the title "Archbishop of the English Nation," and from him all later Archbishops of Canterbury are traced.

Bede tells us that Gregory, not yet Pope, was passing through the local market one day when his wandering glance fell on some blond, blue-eyed captives taken in the northern wars and sent as slaves to Rome. Inquiring after these golden creatures ("those lovely lads," those "wet-fresh windfalls of war's storms," Hopkins calls them) he is told that they are Angles. "Non Angli sed Angeli," he replied; "Not Angles, but Angels." And, as soon as Gregory becomes Pope, the top item on the Roman agenda becomes the conversion of Britain. According to Bede, he even tells the monks he longed to be working beside them there.

The moral result of this physical beauty is what Hopkins wishes to stress in his poem. But, as Ms. Kitchen reminds us, "Had they not been golden-haired and blue-eyed, Hopkins suggests, Gregory might not have noticed them and therefore not concerned himself with converting Britain." (A shocking, but delicious thought!) It was Gregory's appreciative glance, Hopkins is saying, which permitted Britain to transcend the worship of "block or barren stone" and receive "God's better beauty, grace" through the opportunity to embrace Christianity. The glance, and the physical beauty that prompted it, were thus both of divine origin.

The poem is worth further study, for in it Hopkins has some remarkably self-revelatory lines. He argues that we lawfully love what is worthiest of love, and what is the world's loveliest is the selves of men. Yet this "self flashes off frame and face," and we must own that, as "heaven's sweet gift." How then does a gay Jesuit in Victoria's Britain handle that? "Merely meet it...then leave, let that alone." That he has to remind himself, persuade himself, convince himself, force himself to do that, argues Ms. Kitchen, suggests that Hopkins was, after many years a celibate priest, still "vulnerably susceptible" to the attractions of persons of his own sex.

So much for Hopkins; what about us? Well, for openers, if Gregory the Great hadn't been turned on by blue-eyed blonds, we'd still be worshipping with the Druids. If these hunky troopers, those presumably scantily clad Angle P.O.W.'s, hadn't engendered the desire to bring more of the same into

Gregory's orbit (ecclesiastical or other), there'd have been no mission to Kent and therefore no St. Augustine of Canterbury, first Archbishop thereof. And, if no Archbishops of Canterbury, Robert Runcie wouldn't be making ex cathedra pronouncements about gays being "handicapped." He'd be too busy scratching a living raising pigs and, betimes, painting himself blue.

Every Episcopalian, and most lesser breeds, knows why we have a Church of England. That indisputably straight whoremaster, Harry the Eight, had the hots for one Anne Boleyn, n'est-ce pas ? None of our far-flung and diverse Anglican communicants considers himself or herself any the less Christian, or the Anglican church any the less a true church, because of that inconvenient historical fact. Indeed, if one were to look only to its Reformation context, the Church of England might too easily be interpreted as conveying God's particular blessing on macho Protestant heterosexuality.

Many of us would maintain, however, that the fundamental religious change so far as the Church of England and its derivations are concerned is not the transition from Roman to Anglican Catholicism, but rather from paganism to Christianity in England. Looked at in that light, if it hadn't been for one of those fag saints not yet expelled from the calendar by the Moron Majority, no Episcopalian - gay, straight, homophile, or homophobe - would be able to recite the Creed affirming membership in "one, holy, catholic and apostolic church."

The collect for the feast of St. Gregory the Great thanks "Almighty and merciful God, who...didst inspire him to send missionaries to preach the Gospel to the English people...." The unprecedented ecumenical gathering (three-quarters of a billion people) gathered around the altar of St. Paul's Cathedral in person or via satellite television on July 29th for the wedding of the Prince and Princess of Wales, to take only one example, is not a half-bad outcome of a God-inspired glance of appreciation cast at a couple of God-created blue-eyed blonds who set the blood of others dancing nearly 1400 years ago.

Bloody Hands, Clean Consciences (1975)

A short time ago the *Boston Globe* ran a piece on its op-ed page entitled "Shriver Spins All His Wheels," by George F. Will. Kennedy brother-in-law Sargent Shriver was presented as a "squeaky-clean" figure with "unimpeachable liberal credentials," all the right ideological convictions, and appropriate moral intensity. Will thinks Shriver deserves a shot at the Presidency for a variety of reasons including "the pluck he showed in walking the plank with George McGovern in 1972."

One person's pluck is another person's opportunism, of course. Gays looking in this direction for a duly accredited Moses who will lead them into the promised land rather than off the end of another plank had better take a long look at a book by Paul Spike issued by that most reputable of publishers, Alfred A. Knopf, in 1973 under the excessively obscure title *Photographs of My Father*.

Paul Spike's father was the Rev. Dr. Robert W. Spike, who in my salad days was minister of the Judson Memorial Church in Greenwich Village, where he knew Allan Ginsberg, among others. Later he became first Director of the National Council of Churches' Commission on Religion and Race, mobilizer of white church support for Martin Luther King's 1963 March on Washington and for the Selma demonstrations, and foremost Protestant lobbyist for the Civil Rights Act of 1964, the one Bella Abzug and others are now trying to extend to include gays. Bob Spike, for many of us in the '50's and early '60's, was a model of vision and leadership, a pragmatic Christian existentialist who brought religious values out of the pulpit and into the streets. Bob Spike was bisexual, though of course we didn't know it then. Bob Spike was also bludgeoned to death in Columbus, Ohio on Oct. 17, 1966; the instrument of death was a hammer (Spike - get it?).

Paul Spike deeply loved his father, and was deeply loved and supported by him. Paul was puzzled to discover, in a letter to his father from a friend, reference to the Mattachine Society, and the word "Love" used as a close. Another mutual friend, a clergyman, tried to get Paul to go to bed with him, and to encourage this told him that his father was bisexual and Paul was queer too (he isn't). Paul never understood his father's bisexuality, but loved him anyway. More than that, he never understood his death.

Bob Spike's body was discovered clad only in a raincoat. A set of "pornographic magazines" and a list of "suspect" bars in Columbus were found with him, in spite of the fact that he was in town only on Sunday (to preach the dedication sermon at Ohio State's new Christian Center), when both bars and porn shops in Columbus were closed. The police in their "investigations" were careful to leak these "clues" to the newspapers, to tell all his friends whom they questioned that Bob Spike was "a homosexual," and to inform the National Council of Churches' attorney that police surveillance in New York and Washington had yielded evidence of Spike's homosexual activity.

Why police surveillance, and by whom ordered? Bob Spike was a Congregationalist minister who had never joined anything more radical than Americans for Democratic Action. Yet he had put himself on the line among the blacks of Mississippi at a time when Northern civil rights workers and native blacks were regularly getting harassed and even murdered. In the fall of 1966, Spike and others had been trying to prevent the closing down (on charges of "misuse of government funds") of the Child Development Group of Mississippi (CDGM), a program funded by the Office of Economic Opportunity, then headed by Sargent Shriver. At that time, the Johnson administration desperately needed the cooperation of Mississippi Senator John Stennis, of the Armed Services and Appropriations Committees, in order to escalate the Vietnam War by stealth. Lyndon was prepared to deal with Stennis by selling out the Mississippi blacks, as he had done at the 1964 nominating convention, with Hubert Humphrey's cooperation.

Spike, just back from a fact-finding trip to Mississippi which had showed the charges against the child development group to be trumped-up, had an interview with Shriver, whom he later described to his son as "Johnson's hatchet man" and "one of the nastiest men I ever met." In the course of a stormy interview Shriver told Spike "The FBI knows about you, Rev. Spike." And indeed Spike's phone had begun to be tapped again when he had surfaced as leader of the opposition to the CDGM closeout, an experience which he described to Paul as "the dirtiest fight of my life."

The day news of Bob Spike's murder was broadcast (Oct. 18, 1966), news programs also carried the following: "In Washington, Sargent Shriver...has criticized clergymen who want to interfere in the domestic programs of the Federal government. Shriver said 'I am shocked to find some clergymen resorting to character assassination tactics to protest an administrative decision.'"

In the aftermath of Bob Spike's death there were a number of weird and unusual happenings and coincidences, which when the book was published two years ago might have been too easily dismissed (by me, among others) only as confirming the rampant paranoia of the radical counterculture. Evidence of illegal and uncontrolled FBI and CIA activity surfacing in recent months, however, makes Paul Spike's tenuous and non-judgmental statements about them credible to the point where an independent investigation should be made, perhaps using the power of the new Freedom of Information Act. Among these, the most serious are statements possibly linking Spike's murder to the CIA.

The circumstances surrounding Bob Spike's officially "unsolved" murder are murky enough to this day, but two things are clear. One is that Sargent Shriver, "squeaky-clean" Kennedy-Johnson liberal, was using FBI investigative files (material which Paul Spike believes relates to his father's homosexual behavior) to try to pressure (blackmail?) Spike and possibly others into backing off from publicizing the results of their investigation. The other is Shriver's veiled threat of fag-baiting to discredit a full investigation of the facts of the CDGM program, the same tactic used by Columbus police to ward off investigation by responsible church officials into what at this remove appears to be a calculated police cover-up.

If Sargent Shriver comes to your town with his "unimpeachable liberal credentials," I suggest that he be questioned on two points. First, let's find out where he stands on gay rights, and particularly on the Abzug amendment to the historic Civil Rights Act of 1964, which in some sense is a memorial to one of our own. And second, ask him what he knows about events in the fall of 1966 leading to the death of the Rev. Robert W. Spike - bisexual, crusader for minority rights before it became fashionable, man of God, seeker after an earthly kingdom of justice and love.

NOTE (1989): The mystery of Bob Spike's murder has never been officially solved. In a bizarre religious-homophobic footnote, a few years after this essay was written a lesbian working in one of the major denominational agencies (United Methodist, as I recall) was dismissed from her post following disclosure of her sexual orientation. One of the projects terminated with her departure was an investigation into the matter of Bob Spike's murder, using the Freedom of Information Act to solicit Federal government records.

"Saints Preserve Us!" (1987)

On June 5, 1987, the Integrity national convention in St. Louis elected St. Aelred of Rievaulx the patron saint of this national organization of gay Episcopalians and their friends. Aelred of Rievaulx (1110-1167) was an English monk, and the abbot of an important Cistercian monastery in the age of Henry II and Becket, Heloise and Abelard. He is also one of the few medieval thinkers we know unequivocally to have been a self-accepting gay man.

A celibate monk from the age of 24 onward, Aelred built on his experience as a gay man to formulate a theology of community-building and of the love of God and one another in this life which resonates still. By his own account, Aelred was "captivated" by his fellow students, first in a series of schoolboy crushes and then in genital sex. "In writing to his sister," says John Boswell in *Christianity, Social Tolerance and Homosexuality*, "Aelred speaks of this as a time when she held on to her virtue and he lost his."

Later he apparently settled down with one lover, whose friendship he describes as "sweeter to me than all the sweet things of my life." From 1130 to 1134 he was High Steward for King David of Scotland and guardian of the king's son and stepson. In 1134 Aelred entered the Abbey of Rievaulx, in Yorkshire, as a novice, subsequently becoming master of novices there, then Abbot of Revesby. For the final twenty years of his life he was Abbot of Rievaulx itself. He also became the most prominent Cistercian of his day after Bernard of Clairvaux.

As a monk, Aelred had undertaken to renounce genital sex and honored that commitment. But he did not reject love, even passion, between same-sex friends. From his own writings we learn that he was deeply in love with two fellow monks. First was one Simon, who though the Cistercians observed a rule of silence, conveyed his feelings toward the new novice Aelred in body language: "his face spoke to me, his bearing spoke to me, his silence talked." This flame ignited quickly, and burned till Simon's death.

Later Aelred fell in love with an unnamed younger monk, and that relationship developed gradually until "I deemed my heart in a fashion his, and his mine, and he felt in like manner towards me.... Was it not a foretaste of blessedness thus to love and to be loved?" In open opposition to the mainstream monastic tradition, which rejected both the theory and the practice of "special friendships," Aelred saw special same-sex friendships as stepping-stones to the love of God.

As Abbot of Rievaulx he encouraged his monks in non-genital but physical modes of same-sex affection: holding hands, hugging, "spiritual kissing," and even sleeping side by side. In other monasteries, a monk caught taking a brother monk's hand could be expelled. But for Aelred, even if two monks slipped into a carnal relationship, that experience could still be used in a teaching mode, as a step toward a higher relationship. To express love for a "significant other" was not evil, but to express it within the context of the greater love of God was the highest good.

Aelred wrote several treatises, apparently read if not accepted within the mainstream church tradition. In "On Spiritual Friendship" he even explores the implications of mouth-to-mouth kissing as a spiritual exercise. "Special friendships" thus involve "the kiss of Christ, who breathes his holy affection into those who really love each other, and who leads such friends to the kiss of mystical union." Incendiary stuff, in those days!

In his "Mirror of Charity" Aelred distills his whole theology into three simple words: "God is friendship." He realized the complexity of friendship, involving as it does spontaneous affection towards some and not others, the stimulus of physical attractiveness, intellectual affinity, erotic attraction, and spiritual union. And he simply vaults over the anti-gay chain of ecclesiastical attitude from St Augustine onward to justify his doctrine by the example of Jesus and John, "the disciple whom Jesus loved," and who had lain on his breast, in a relationship Aelred termed a "marriage." Clearly these are the writings of a gay man who has loved and been the recipient of love from other men, and found peace, reconciliation, security, and serenity in that blessed state. Gay and Proud? Well, very nearly.

Aelred's writings and character attracted many others, probably many primarily same-gender oriented men among them, to his monastery and order, including the previously mentioned stepson of the King of Scotland. While Aelred was Abbot, the monastery at Rievaulx housed 150 monks and 500 lay brothers, a total exceeded by no other English monastery of his day. Five sister abbeys in England were founded under his leadership. And because his treatises originated as talks to his community, we know that some of the most healing and comforting words in all of medieval English history were spoken to the monks and brothers of this abbey in the twenty years their kindly and reflective leader shared with them his ideal vision of Christian friendship and his idealization of love between men.

After Aelred's death a local cult grew up around his veneration, and in 1476 the Cistercians began celebrating a feast day in his name. The Catholic Church in Rome has never formally canonized him, and now that he is recognized as a "gay saint" is not likely to do so. But the Episcopal Church in the U.S., which differs from Rome both in its definition of sainthood (as "witness to the faith," not as "miracle-worker") and in its manner of selection, placed Aelred on its liturgical calendar during its 1985 General Convention. During the debate the Bishop of Newark expressly pointed out Aelred's homosexual orientation, and knowing this, the Convention voted him through anyway.

Part of the Collect approved for the Feast of St. Aelred (Jan. 12th) is worth quoting here. "Pour into our hearts, O God, the Holy Spirit's gift of love, that we, clasping each other's hand, may share the joy of friendship, human and divine, and with your servant Aelred draw many into your community of love...."

John Boswell says of Aelred that he "gave love between those of the same gender its most powerful and lasting expression in a Christian context." But one need not be Christian, or even Episcopalian ("God's frozen people") to take from that prayer the ideals of the outstretched hand, same-sex friendships, and the loving community, and put them to good use in our troubled society. Aelred thus stands as an important icon. But he is only one of the many gay men and women in history whose example encourages us to create a richer human existence for ourselves and for all those whose lives we in turn may touch through the living out in community of our highest values and aspirations.

Part Six:
Gay Landscapes

Franciscan Odyssey (1987)

One gets through the last stages of snowy New England winters only by visualizing sunnier landscapes where one has been and, *deo volente*, will some day be again. Such a place is Assisi, high in the Umbrian hills. As we approached it by train on a mid-April day, we could see why St. Francis thought the upper Spoleto valley to be the most beautiful spot on earth.

At the station we caught a bus which took us up the hill to the edge of town. We got directions from the bus driver (who must be used to execrable American manglings of his beautiful native tongue), and climbed the narrow zig-zag street past the basilica to our hotel on the Via San Francesco. We had come in search of the saint on his own turf, my lover because he is a devout Roman Catholic and a third-order Franciscan, and I for more diverse reasons: religious, ecological, artistic, and not least because if Francesco d'Assisi wasn't gay, my antennae have rusted with age. The Franciscan recruiting poster in the basilica shows a sexy, androgynous young Italian guy in a simple brown robe; if they ever hung it in a gay bar, their quota would be filled instantly.

And why not? This gentle founder of a medieval band of brothers was part of a broader gay tradition of opting for a more humane way in the midst of a barbarian society which, like our own, was obsessed with war, money-grubbing and baby-making. The monastic calling, as well as calls to teaching, healing, the cure of the terminally ill and ministry to the outcasts of society (for example, lepers in the Middle Ages), have all appealed to gay people in Francis' day and ever since for similar life-affirming reasons.

Over the ensuing couple of days we explored the town, beginning with the transcendentally beautiful upper basilica containing Giotto's frescoes depicting the life of St. Francis. Recently restored, although with some irrecoverable sections, these frescoes seem freshly painted. No doubt others will disagree, but in my view the early Renaissance (and then only in certain Italian cities) yielded religious art of a worthiness not seen in that genre before or since. The difference, I think, is in the handling of the human body; not just the technical handling, but the valuing of it. The Giotto frescoes are a particularly happy way of teaching the life of this appealing saint, who was such an attraction for young men in his own lifetime and who continues to be so, both in the Roman and Anglican traditions.

The old town itself is superb, with vistas both of distant landscapes and of an urban fabric of medieval and Renaissance streetscapes still in lively daily use. Assisi, like its sister city San Francisco, is a very up-and-down place, and we ended each day on tottering legs. We saw many of the specific sites associated with Francis' life, including the public square where he stripped naked as a declaration of independence from his rich father's bounty.

At the far end of the old town we visited the basilica of his counterpart St. Clare, to whom he extended coordinate status as the foundress of a Franciscan order of sisters. We lunched in a bar which had originally been a house of refreshment for medieval pilgrims, and viewed the pictures in the municipal gallery, including some springlike paintings by a local artist hitherto unknown to me, Tiberio of Assisi. One evening we had dinner in a former textile warehouse (or perhaps a stable), our meal washed down with the local white wine, Blanco d'Assisi, which I heartily recommend.

The gay ambience surrounding St. Francis is depicted for us in modern dress (as it were) by our bisexual brother Franco Zeffirelli in his rather sentimental film "Brother Sun, Sister Moon" (1972), which used to be shown regularly in repertory film houses before those were largely wiped out by the VCR revolution. The film is now available on videocassette, and it is occasionally shown on television. I recommend making an effort to see it, both for the scenery and the homoerotic ambience permeating the story. (The British actor playing Francesco isn't hard on the eyes, either.)

Beyond the sentiment, the scenery, Donovan's settings of Francis' prayers, and the good-looking guys in the film lies an important message which gay people may take to heart. Even in this more open day, we all learn early that the appearances assigned us commonly mask the reality within. There used to be a gay liberation button to this effect: "How Dare You Presume I'm Heterosexual." But of course, everybody does, at least at the start.

Francis penetrated and transformed that appearance/reality dualism. The realities beneath the deformed, the leper, the fatuously powerful, the self-important were all discovered and revalued in terms which presuppose very different criteria of human worth from those we normally assume. Even the medieval world-view itself, which saw the world as an evil and fearsome place, was transformed in the thought of Francis of Assisi. To him, the world was a place of beauty and light, containing the wonders of the incarnate natural order and the goodness of God's creation. That's as radical a rejection of the mainstream view as anyone could make in medieval Europe. Can we learn to see the value of things with equal penetration, accustomed as gay folk are from puberty (if not before) to the lived experience of the appearance/reality problem?

The glorious light of the upper church at Assisi plays off against our own lives, as we see our world in rather darker terms than we did just a decade ago. Yet the task of doing the work we are now called to do is made more hopeful by the work of Francis and his imitators down the centuries: "...Where there is hatred, let us sow love...where there is despair, hope...where there is darkness, light; where there is sadness, joy."

The question is not "did he or didn't he," so often unanswerable in gay history. The point is that Francis created two co-ordinate homosocial communities, one for men and one for women, which held up the notion of a family of choice and free association and used it to reach out to the wanderer, the person who is "different," the homeless, the needy, the sick, and the dying. In the age of AIDS we might at least think of making Francesco d'Assisi an honorary gay saint.

A Sicilian Fantasy (1984)

At the international photo show in Amsterdam earlier this summer, the most striking section was that devoted to images of man, *au naturel*. A number of outstanding Dutch and other European photographers contributed. This particular exhibit seemed to attract the most attention, from gay and non-gay alike, and deservedly so. It certainly did from me.

The photos were preceded by a panel which briefly set them in art-historical context. Included were examples of classic Greek sculpture, Michelangelo's "David," and two photographs of nude youths by the Baron Wilhelm von Gloeden, native of Germany, Sicilian expatriate, and latter-day gay cultural hero.

Von Gloeden was born in 1856, grew up at the courts of Schwerin and Berlin, and became a student both of painting and of the culture of ancient Greece. In the late 1870's he was told by Berlin doctors that he had "consumption," and, in accordance with the medical theories of that day, was advised to seek out a warmer and drier climate. Chancing to meet another German artist who had "discovered" Taormina some years before, von Gloeden decided to settle in this beautiful and then isolated town high above the eastern coast of Sicily, with its breathtaking views of Mt. Etna and the Ionian Sea. Except for a period during World War I when, as an enemy alien, he was forced to return to Germany to avoid imprisonment, he remained there for the next fifty years.

In Taormina Wilhelm's health improved, and his first villa, in the street of the Greek theater (still an impressive classical site), became a visitor center for male friends in the upper reaches of German society. During the early 1880's, while on a trip to Naples, he stayed with a cousin who had become a skilled photographer. Von Gloeden was fascinated by this relatively new and tremendously complex activity, which he first regarded as a hobby or sideline. Later, when the young artist was caught by family financial reverses, his childhood friend the Grand Duke of Mecklenburg (a "soul brother") sent him a huge camera and set of glass plates. Von Gloeden soon discovered that his photographs of landscapes and townscapes, skillfully done, could be a source of income.

In addition to its natural beauty, its climate, and its range of interesting architecture from Greek times onward, Taormina was and is noted for its culturally diverse and often physically attractive population, especially its male youth. Von Gloeden's charm and courtly manners quickly made him popular among the simple townsfolk. His homosexual tastes and the contacts of a faithful houseboy opened to him and his friends a series of encounters with young men who were available in the evenings both for villa parties and for excursions to the bosky meadows of Monte Ziretto, on the outskirts of town.

The combination of all these influences moved von Gloeden to create his celebrated series of some 3000 glass-plate negatives, many of nude or lightly draped youths (along with some females) in various classical poses and settings. In this way he forged a romantic link with the town's earliest culture, that of Magna Graecia. Albumen prints and postcards of his more sedate photos were purchased by the growing number of visitors to Taormina as well as by libraries and collectors elsewhere, some winding up as illustrations in the *National Geographic*. Von Gloeden's photographs also won awards at a number of international art exhibitions, attracting other photographers to Taormina for what we may hope were enjoyable visits. And, as a result of the circulation of his less inhibited photographs among the appropriate underground, Taormina attracted an international clientele of gay tourists and permanent settlers, some of whom built villas of their own in this hospitable community.

Von Gloeden's relationships with his models, the last of whom died only in 1977, were often sexual but seldom exploitative. In the normal cycle of development, as in ancient Greece, the youth would marry; if the spouse-to-be came from a poor family, the Baron might provide the dowry. Also, each model had a place in von Gloeden's account books, since he set aside part of the income from each photo as a royalty for the subject. In this way, when the boy married, the money was there for him to buy a fishing boat, or set up in a trade, or start a business or guest house.

In the mid-1930's Benito Mussolini's Fascist goons smashed over a thousand of von Gloeden's glass plate negatives. Upwards of another thousand were lost in various ways during World War II. A few were preserved by a Taormina peasant and his wife under the floor of their simple home to prevent government seizure and destruction. For some time after the war the hand of censorship lay heavily in Sicily, and von Gloeden's images could be obtained only surreptitiously.

Nowadays, though, the situation has changed radically. Reproductions of the Baron's photos, in print or postcard form, are freely sold in the shops along the Corso Umberto, Taormina's main business street. Both of the town's bookstores, last April, displayed in the center of their front windows an Italian book on von Gloeden's work, featuring a nude boy on the cover. This, of course, would earn bookstore proprietors a rock through the plate glass in Boston.

It is an American gay fantasy that all Italian boys are both beautiful and available. Clearly, however, the proportion of attractive youth seems higher in Taormina than in any gay rendezvous I've seen, from San Francisco to Athens. The local ambience is a remarkable demonstration of the persistence of the past in the present. This is true both because physical features derived from Greek, Norman, Arab and other origins are all represented in living replicas, and because the hang-out spots for the local youths are often the same in which von Gloeden photographed their ancestors upwards of a century ago. I like it.

Von Gloeden's remains rest in Taormina's little Protestant cemetery, on a hill-slope overlooking the sea, and next to the Catholic cemetery in which his models are buried. The Protestant cemetery is now little used and rather overgrown. When I explored it, passing en route a beautiful example of the local fauna "just resting" against a nearby auto, I had to sweep through the area twice before I found the Baron's grave. This detailed survey also showed me that there is definitely a disproportionately high percentage of foreign-born single men buried here.

The marker is a simple white marble cross, inscribed only "Guglielmo von Gloeden. Nato 16-9-1856. Morto 16-2-1931." Appropriately enough, a photo of the Baron is mounted in a heavy metal frame just below the inscription. I was pleased to learn from this pious pilgrimage that von Gloeden has not been forgotten in Taormina. As is often the case in the

Mediterranean, there is a flower bowl in front of the marker. And very recently, probably on Easter Sunday two days before, someone had placed in this bowl a single carnation. It was red, symbol of the living, rather than the white of the dead.

American gay awareness of von Gloeden and his work was rekindled through an article by David Loo published during the "Stonewall summer" of 1969 in the now-defunct gay male magazine *Queen's Quarterly* (really!). Thanks to Charles Leslie's *Wilhelm von Gloeden: Photographer* (1977) and other recent books which both enlarge our knowledge of the man and reproduce his once-verboten photographs, we are beginning to see in this pioneer artist a major figure in our truly marvelous gay cultural history.

"N Neapolitan Journey (1985)

aples... noisy as pandemonium day and night," wrote Arthur Riggs in a 1916 *National Geographic*. [It is] "peopled by a conglomerate mass as strikingly beautiful physically as they are notoriously untrustworthy."

Arriving there in April, 1984 after a long and exhausting train trip from Taormina, I was somewhat apprehensive because of just that sort of description. Much to my surprise, the next five days were so filled with rich sensory impressions that I found my stay there among the most rewarding of my two months abroad that year. One of the master images I retain is that of the persistence of classical ideals of male beauty and conduct embedded in the daily experience of the otherwise tawdry present.

Neither here nor elsewhere in Italy did I replicate Alfred C. Kinsey's experience during a 1955 visit. Kinsey had found that although in Rome the bellboys were satisfied with a tip, those in Naples "might sit down and make it clear they would be glad to stay for other purposes." Somewhat to my disappointment, I was shown to my hotel room by a middle-aged bellboy in the conventional manner.

After a comfortable bath, food and ten hours of sleep, I set out for the Museo Archeologico off the Via Roma to see the great Farnese collection and other examples of classical sculpture. Highlights included a Roman copy of the famous Athenian statue of the lovers Harmodios and

Aristogeiton, the latter a full-grown man with beard and the former a beautifully formed ephebe. The museum was a treasure-trove of gay impressions; a bronze ephebe, a Doryphoros from Pompeii which is said to represent the most perfect (and rather butch) male proportions in the classical canon, a Ganymede with eagle (symbol of Zeus), an outsize nude warrior (from the Baths of Caracalla) carrying his dead son over his shoulder, and of course the muscle-bound Farnese Hercules and the grossly overblown Farnese bull group. But one can spend hours there also with the bronzes, portrait busts, mosaics and Pompeiian frescoes. I was overwhelmed.

Thus fortified by the classical sense of bodily proportion, I went out into the streets to see it replicated. It was sheer joy to walk down the Via Roma, the "Main Street" (and principal hustling street) of Naples, with half the street signs missing, past shabby Baroque buildings, in the midst of unbelievable traffic and street noise. Pandemonium indeed! Yet above all I found myself rejoicing in the incredible vitality of the life of the city on an April afternoon.

Naples derives its name from Neapolis, a 6th century (B.C.) Greek settlement. The Romans conquered it in 326 B.C., but for several centuries thereafter Greek remained the official language and Greek ways of life persisted. Naples became a center of learning for Roman youth, and famous musical and gymnastic contests were held there. The geographer Strabo tells us that "the Greek mode of life at Neapolis finds special favor with the men who make their living by educating the young...." Paul Goodman would have loved it.

One of the great occurrences in the education of young Americans forty years ago was wartime Naples, described in semi-fictional form by John Horne Burns in his novel *The Gallery* (1947). Set primarily in the Galleria Umberto, a late 19th century arcade, in August, 1944, the book includes a vivid description of a 1940's gay bar favored by Allied military and Italian gays. Burns also manages to catch the larger lessons of this wartime exposure to profound cultural differences concerning love and custom.

The Galleria Umberto remained a prime cruising area through Kinsey's visit in the mid 'fifties. My own "pilgrimage" to this gay historic site disclosed a lot of young males hanging around (as anywhere in Naples). It also suggested that the Galleria has more recently been yuppified, rather like Boston's Quincy Market,

That afternoon, after a research visit to the archives of the world-renowned Naples Zoological Station, I passed through the nearby Piazza Vittoria, a center for gay bars and late-night cruising, according to my

Spartacus guidebook. What was striking about the daytime view was the several outdoor reproductions of classic nude male statues, all in a row, as if giving their blessing to the whole enterprise. Indeed, I was struck by the large number of nude male images around the city, outdoors as well as in museums. One would like to think that growing up with these (as opposed to the baggy-pants clergy, reformers and politicians of Boston's public art) makes the Neapolitans both more comfortable with their own bodies and more in touch with their classical heritage.

Certainly the physicality of the Neapolitan male is expressed more freely than with us. Thomas Belmonte, a Columbia graduate student in anthropology, did a participant-observer study of a poor neighborhood of Naples, published as *The Broken Fountain* (1979). He got to know a number of young men and youths from poor families, and found himself encouraged (in one case by the mother of a fifteen-year-old) to sleep with them. They were borderline petty thieves and part-time hustlers for the most part, but this wasn't (so far as we are told) a sexual thing. Rather, "to sleep beside another meant to trust and to care," Belmonte writes. "It was a way of reassuring someone that you were there for them."

Similarly, I saw many men enarming each other, or just naturally putting an arm around another man's shoulder, or kissing one another on arrival or departure in train stations. It's the result of a wholly different history, and the actions are not emotionally supercharged, as with us. I liked it; to my mind it shows a far saner way of coping with issues of the body and with sexual energies than Americans customarily exhibit.

On my last day in Naples I visited several churches, including the Gothic cathedral, which encloses a fourth century Early Christian basilica remodelled in the thirteenth century and Baroquified in the seventeenth. Its 27 columns, however, are probably those of a classical temple of Apollo on this same site, an extraordinary example of the persistence of Greek culture from the era of Neapolis to the present day.

Catching a taxi from my hotel to the train station, I got caught in a massive traffic jam, ran the last few hundred yards (with luggage), and made my compartment on the Paris express with four minutes to spare. Still agitated, I discovered (using my tourist Italian) that the *carozza ristorante* would not appear until we reached Rome. My equilibrium was both restored and disturbed anew when a beautiful Neapolitan youth appeared carrying a basket of sandwiches and cold drinks. He remained a bit longer than was necessary to make the sale. And I knew that, some day, I shall return to this corrupt, polluted and thoroughly appealing corner of the world. Strabo was right: Neapolis still finds special favor with those of us who make our livings by educating the young.

Sounding The Sirens (1984)

I have never been an aficionado of popular music, but occasionally bits of something I heard in my misspent youth are haltingly recalled in middle-aged tranquility. So it is with "The Isle of Capri," which I recall as some sort of hymn to heterosexual honeymooning or similar pagan rite. Although I may have had some earlier inkling of it, I didn't get the gay goods on Capri until, some years ago, I discovered and read Roger Peyrefitte's romantic novel, *The Exile of Capri*.

Strictly as novel, *The Exile of Capri* is distinguished neither for plot nor for characterization. It simply follows the life history of a real French nobleman and third-rate litterateur, Count Jacques d'Adelswärd-Fersen. Fersen had visited Capri as a young man, and returned there in 1904 after being convicted of debauching the morals of several schoolboys. The scandal surrounded his so-called "pink masses," featuring scantily clad youths and their admirers, erotic poetry and dramatic tableaux set to music by gay composers such as Reynaldo Hahn. Indeed, one might appropriately characterize these musical occasions as a clear case of sowing one's wild notes. (Let's hear it for the lowest form of humor!)

The island of Capri was then, and remained for a long time, a center of attraction for the upper-class European, English and even American lesbian and gay underground. All kinds of gay characters, major and minor, appear on Peyrefitte's pages. Among the best known today are Oscar Wilde, the English travel writer Norman Douglas, and the German armaments maker Friedrich von Krupp. Krupp, who built a scenic roadway called the Via Krupp now frequented nightly by rent-boys and their lease-holders, committed suicide when a Socialist journalist seeking political advantage made an issue of Krupp's homosexual activities on Capri.

Names of a generous assortment of minor gay German royalty, French lesbian nobility, English gentry and American expatriates course through Peyrefitte's pages. Americans include the Messrs. Jackson and Woodcock, once youthful clerks in the American consulate at Stuttgart. They had become lovers of King Karl of Württemburg, who in his kingly power made them counts of that south German realm. They also include the wealthy "sisters" Wolcott-Perry, permanent residents of Capri (and now buried there), one of whose birth names was Wolcott and the other Perry. Peyrefitte even draws in a discussion of the work of the German gay sex researcher Dr. Magnus Hirschfeld, known among the congnoscenti as "Aunt Magnesia."

Why Capri? The island has a long history of sexual tolerance, based to some degree on economics and also in tradition. There were tales long ago told, by the gossipy Suetonius and others, of the paederistic proclivities of the Emperor Tiberius, who retired to Capri to build a dozen pleasure-palaces. And a French traveller in the 1630's noted in his diary, subsequently published, that at what is now Anacapri "both the women and the young boys greatly enjoy love-making." But it was the naming in 1826 of the famous "Blue Grotto" (later popularized in a novel by the gay Danish storyteller Hans Christian Andersen) which began the serious scenic and touristic attraction of the island for Northern Europeans.

This, in turn, eventually led individual travellers to explore the island's numerous and varicolored marine grottoes, rowed there by youthful fisher-boys who were open to further exploration. Or the visitors ascended Capri's mountains by muleback to see its Roman ruins, in the company of young, handsome, and willing muleteers. Thus when Peyrefitte tells us that young Prince Leopold of Hohenzollern "celebrated his twenty-fifth birthday beneath the vaulting of a Capriot grotto," it would not do to suppose that he was there solely to study the island's intricate geological formations.

Settlers and exiles, like Count Fersen and Norman Douglas, built or bought villas of their own and settled in with youthful Italian companions, often masquerading as "servants." These would, upon reaching an appropriate age, most often marry and found families, aided by a gift or subsidy from their former patron. This pattern, founded on a realistic appraisal of what fueled the tourist economy, brought the locals here, as in Taormina, to an ungrudging acceptance of the wealthy gay traveller and resident.

After the Blue Grotto, today's most popular visitor site on the island is Villa San Michele at Anacapri. This unusual house was built by an eccentric Swedish doctor, Axel Munthe, said by Peyrefitte to be the illegitimate half-brother of King Gustav V of Sweden (d. 1950). There is certainly a strong physical resemblance, and Munthe lived at the Royal Palace in Stockholm until his death in 1949. Munthe was personal physician to Gustav's ailing Queen, who spent most of her time on Capri before she died in 1930. The King and his brothers were also frequent visitors to the island though, Peyrefitte tells us, Gustav spent most of his time "at the Café Morgano [where muleteers and fishermen mingled with princes] when he was not in the grottoes." (King Gustav, who lived to be ninety-two, in his old age had a young Swedish guardsman detailed to his bed each night to keep him warm. What a wonderful energy-saving substitute for an electric blanket!)

Munthe's home, now a museum and residence for Swedish artists, scholars and writers, is on a site earlier chosen by Tiberius for one of his own villas. The views of the sea from its terraces are superb. The house is set in the midst of a lovely garden, and Munthe's collection of real and fake antiquities is engagingly set in walls and niches inside and out. In his baronial bedroom there are no less than three bronzes of nude ephebes, with a fourth depicted in bas-relief. "Even though twice briefly married and with children," says my travel diary, "it appears the good doctor was not beyond captivation by the special charms of Capri."

The island remains charming, even under assault by today's mass tourism. To be sure, the mules which used to carry travellers over the hills to Tiberius' Villa Jovis are long gone, and with them the muleteers; by the time I got back from a climb no one my age and physical condition should undertake on a hot day, I longed for the services of both. As I sat later that afternoon recovering at an outdoor cafe in the Piazzetta, or Town Square, I rested my eyes both on the scenic vista before me and on the current crop of attractive ephebes, who in turn were hanging over the terrace railings and eyeballing the tourists. Thus I found myself linked to Wilde and Douglas and Krupp and Fersen and all the others.

Sailing out on the Capri boat from the Naples mole, the last thing one passes is a statue mounted on the end of the breakwater. It is St. Januarius, Patron of Naples, his hand extended in blessing to the pious fishermen and sailors who cast themselves upon the mercies of the Tyrrhenian Sea. At the end of the day, as one leaves the Marina Grande, the principal harbor of Capri, one sees at the end of that breakwater a group of bronzed and youthful Capriots, arms raised in farewell, yet with the hint of an invitation to return. Norman Douglas was right; here, if anywhere, one truly hears the Sirens sing.

A Bavarian Fantasy (1986)

If memory serves, it was Voltaire who observed that French is the language which should be spoken to the learned, Italian to the beautiful, and German to the geese. I have found French useful in my research, and encountered enough beautiful Italian boys to encourage mastery of a few phrases in that lovely language. But I came too late to German ever to hope for proficiency, as I discovered a few years ago in preparing for my first visit to that country. But if I were free to do so, I'd go back this year, language or no.

This summer the Germans are celebrating a Jubilee Year in commemoration of the lives and creations of two nineteenth century Bavarian kings, Ludwig I (1786-1868) and his gay grandson Ludwig II (1845-1886). Ludwig I, who reigned from 1825 to 1848, rebuilt much of Munich in neo-Classical style. He also assembled the collection of classical artifacts which makes the Munich Glyptothek one of the choicest collections of Greek sculpture outside Athens itself.

Ludwig's grandson, born in August, 1845 on his grandfather's birthday, while still a child enjoyed building with toy bricks and dressing up as a nun. He grew up a dreamy dark-haired and dewy-eyed romantic, becoming King in 1864 when he was barely 18. Ludwig spent much of his early adult life in search of a great "Freund" (which, in German, has a more intimate meaning than "friend," though not necessarily a sexual one). As every opera queen knows, one of his greatest infatuations was Richard Wagner, whose music dramas he championed and whose presence he welcomed in Munich. Wagner, a thoroughgoing opportunist, milked the King's affection for all he could get. But Wagner's political intrigues became an issue for the Bavarian government and Ludwig was forced to ask him to leave Munich, much as his grandfather had done with the pseudo-Spanish dancer Lola Montez, the ultimate cause of Ludwig I's abdication.

Ludwig II was, even in his earlier years, somewhat unstable, and his beautiful auburn-haired, blue-eyed brother Otto, the next heir, was even more so. (My guess is that Otto was also gay, but I can't confirm that.) After publicly announcing his forthcoming marriage to his cousin Sophie, Ludwig suddenly broke the engagement. Some think he did so because he had been forced to confront within himself the fact that his attraction toward men went beyond acceptable ideals of Romantic friendships. At seventeen he had become deeply attached to Prince Paul von Thurn und Taxis, a member of one of Germany's wealthiest princely families. Although this infatuation, like that with Wagner, was probably not sexually expressed, there were rumors in Munich that Ludwig was sexually intimate with his valet. His Master of the Horse and private secretary, Richard Hornig, was probably his first real lover. He also had affairs with the then young and later famous Austrian actor, Josef Kainz, and a number of other men, some of whom we know only by last name.

As Ludwig grew older, physically grosser, and more eccentric, the social standing of his sex partners declined. He often found his later pleasures among good-looking soldiers, whom he encountered on his various royal journeyings and then assigned to his household staff. The phrase "domestic service" took on new meaning as these quasi-literate young troopers and stable-boys were assigned positions as valets and lackeys, sometimes serving as intermediaries between Ludwig and his ministers. After 1871, stories of dissolute nocturnal parties in hunting-lodges and picnics in secluded woodlands began to leak out, involving young men dancing naked with each other, and worse (or, depending on one's point of view, better). It is said that the King commissioned marble statues of his minions, but if so they have unfortunately not survived.

During the Franco-Prussian War (1870) Prince Otto began fading in and out of reality, and a few years later had to be confined permanently in the remote castle of Fürstenreid. Ludwig, distraught over Otto's condition and guilt-ridden over his own sexual activity, withdrew from his public duties and embarked on a fantastic building program, which included three major castles as well as hunting-lodges and other structures. His admiration for Wagner's operas, especially Lohengrin, is reflected in the most famous of these, Neuschwanstein. But he also imitated the grandeur of the Bourbons, with a Grand Trianon-style palace at Linderhof and a replica of Versailles on the island of Herrenchiemsee.

As his construction debts, eccentricities and isolation grew, and on the basis of reports rather than personal examination, Ludwig was diagnosed as insane by Dr. Bernard Gudden, a psychiatric bureaucrat who had been in charge of Otto since 1872. A regency was established under Ludwig's uncle, Prince Luitpold, and the King was seized at Neuschwanstein and taken to the castle of Berg on the Starnberger See. On June 13, 1886 (Whitsunday), Ludwig went out for a walk with Dr. Gudden, now his keeper as well as Otto's, and walked partway into the lake. When Gudden pursued him, Ludwig, now beyond despair and probably perfectly lucid, drowned his doctor and then himself. In a sense, Ludwig had become one of the first gay victims of modern psychiatric labelling.

Otto I reigned in his prison-castle, but because of his madness did not rule, for nearly thirty years. A new Prince-Regent deposed him in 1913 and took the title Ludwig III. But in the eyes of legitimists there were now two kings in Bavaria, and the peasants muttered that no good would come of it. A year later World War I broke out, and at its close revolution erupted in Munich. Ludwig III fled to Switzerland, and the 700-year rule of the House of Wittelsbach was brought to an inglorious conclusion. So much for messing with gays.

This summer gay tourists can visit Ludwig's three fantasy castles, enjoy bed and breakfast where young soldiers stripped naked and danced before the King in his hunting-lodge at Schachen, and pray for the repose of his troubled soul at the Votivkapelle erected by his sorrowing mother, Queen Marie, at the point of land where he stepped off to drown himself and his chief tormenter in the Starnberger See. Perhaps those of us who cannot go to Germany this summer will observe a moment of reflective silence on June 13th in commemoration of this mad, gay, guilt-ridden King whose romantic and fantastic works of art and championship of Wagner's music are now an important part of the received tradition of twentieth century gay sensibility.

Stranger in Paradise (1983)

The oasis of Siwa is in the news again. "Well," you may say, "in the midst of municipal elections and foreign crises and seasonal sports festivals and wet bikini contests, how did I miss that?" The answer is, of course, "quite easily!"

The oasis of Siwa has, nevertheless, been "hot news" for some twenty-five centuries, ever since Herodotos first wrote about it. It is hot news again in archaeological circles because Roxbury Highlands novelist and home rehabber Gary Chafetz, taking his cue from the Father of History, has set out, equipped with state-of-the-art sub-surface scanning devices, on a six month expedition in search of an army lost in the desert near Siwa in about 525 B.C. This 25,000-man force was sent out by the Persian conqueror Cambyses (whom Herodotos properly calls a "senseless madman") to capture Siwa and destroy the oracular shrine of Amun there. Chafetz' search is endorsed by the National Geographic Society, the Egyptian government, and numerous reputable archaeologists, who are persuaded both that Chafetz may well find Cambyses' army and that if he does, it could be one of the more spectacular archaeological finds of the century.

Fans of Mary Renault will recall that Alexander the Great, having captured Egypt from the Persians and laid out the plans for his new city of Alexandria, then made the long and hazardous trek over the desert in 331 B.C to consult the Siwan oracle, which the Greeks understood as a manifestation of Zeus. The journey, which included a sand storm holding up the party for four days, was relieved by a fortunately timed rain shower and, it is alleged, by two snakes who appeared en route to serve as guides, escorting Alexander himself and conversing with him in Greek on the way.

The chief priest of the shrine hailed Alexander as "Son of Zeus," and through there is some dispute about what the King and the oracle had to say to one another, we do know that, years later, Alexander sacrificed to Zeus-Amun at the mouth of the Indus River. And when his lover Hephaestion died at Ecbatana, in Persia, Alexander sent back to the shrine at Siwa to ask how Hephaestion might be honored, as a god or as a hero. Some sources say that, on his own deathbed, Alexander asked that his body be taken to Siwa for burial at the shrine. Evidence about the later history of the oracle is scant, but it may have lasted long enough to be suppressed by the Emperor Justinian, who attempted to stamp out paganism among the oases of Libya at the same time he was trying to stamp out homosexuality back home in Byzantium.

The oasis itself, 350 miles to the west of Cairo, remained a caravan-stop on the date-producing route, unvisited by Westerners from Roman times until 1792. Nineteenth century Western visitors generally appear to have been shocked by what they saw there. In 1896, for instance, a British army officer commented that the Roman rock tombs, until recently, had been "the resort of all that was disreputable in Siwa," and that "from report, Siwan morals are of the lowest." Another scandalized Brit reported that "the morals of either sex are said to overstep all limits of decency." Some German testimony provides a clue to the reasons for these late Victorian reactions: "the feast of marrying a boy was celebrated with great pomp." And the German noted that, though the bride-price of a woman was a little over a pound, that of a boy was fifteen pounds, plus a clothing allowance.

In 1926, a British official accompanied by the Egyptian Minister of the Interior visited Siwa. Coming upon a wedding ceremony, they discovered the groom to be forty and the "bride" to be a fifteen-year-old male. Upon the Minister's return to Cairo, he sent out the Immam of a local mosque to induce the inhabitants of Siwa to forsake their scandalous customs. On his next visit, the Minister came upon another wedding ceremony in progress. This time the happy couple were the Immam himself and a boy of fourteen.

While in Oxford last summer I picked up at Blackwell's a copy of the late gay writer Robin Maugham's book *Search for Nirvana* (1975), which provides some of the juicy details recorded above, and more. It seems that the custom of same-sex marriages arose originally from the fact that no bachelor ("zaggala," in Berber) was permitted to stay within the walls of the town after sunset, for fear he would infiltrate the harems. Instead, the zaggalas lived in little thatched huts outside the gates, and were assigned the role of defenders of the town. Since most of the time there was no defending to do, they would lie about singing and drinking the local palm wine, or "lubki." When a boy reached puberty, he was sent out to join the zaggalas. He would then be courted by one of them, who would pursue him into the palm groves, make love, and bring the beloved back to his shelter. If the boy then consented to a permanent relationship, they would be "married."

During his visit to Siwa some time after World War II, Maugham talked with one such gay couple working as laborers in the outlier oasis of Seiton. And in the guest-house he accidentally found the recently heterosexually married houseman in bed with a lascivious fourteen-year-old male, whom the houseman generously offered to share (Maugham declined).

One evening a seventeen-year-old, dark-eyed Senussi Bedouin named Salem, who had been lost in the desert while on patrol with the Libyan army, showed up at the oasis and was given a room at the guest-house. Robin, then aged 31, was immediately attracted to him. After a shower Salem entered Robin's room clad only in a towel, saying that he had always slept communally, in a tent or in a barracks, and was afraid to sleep alone in his room. The hospitable Robin promptly invited Salem to share his bed. Though Salem feigned sleep, an exploring hand broke the cultural barrier, and they made love until nearly dawn. The next day they visited the shrine of Zeus-Amun together, and enjoyed a torrid four-day romance before Salem had to return to his unit.

On the last night before Robin himself had to leave Siwa, he was entertained at the guest-house by some two dozen zaggalas of various ages. The men and boys danced a traditional Siwan dance for him, to a refrain which says "my love is like a flaming torch, and sometimes I take him to my breast," which, at intervals, some did. As the evening wore on, the lubki flowed freely, and the flute and the drums and the dancers all got wilder. The dancers chanted "Ya Haoul il lah," - "O power of God," while moving to a more explicitly sexual ecstasy, male organs rising to the ready, virility poured out in guilt-free orgasms. It was an elating, yet depressing revelation for the culture-bound Robin Maugham.

The area of desert Chafetz is searching falls within the last fifty miles of the ancient trail between Egyptian Thebes and Siwa. If he hits the jackpot, he will no doubt celebrate first in Siwa itself. One hopes that the zaggalas will dance in celebration of his achievement, and that the international media will once again give some attention to the culture of this remote oasis.

Siwa itself may have as much to teach us as the mummified army of Cambyses. In our own age it is perhaps even more commonplace for senseless madmen to send out military expeditions to enforce ideological conformity. Yet Siwa presents us with the redeeming counterexample of a society which preserved a non-conforming style of same-sex union for longer than words have been set down on paper. Think on it.

NOTE (1989): Gary Chafetz gave two lectures after his return from the Siwa expedition, at the Boston Center for Adult Education, which I eagerly attended. He had found a series of rock cairns *en echelon* pointing toward Siwa which could only have been left by Cambyses' army, but little else, and certainly no great treasure. Siwa itself, however, is probably the more fruitful venue for future archaeological research. (Not to mention future gay anthropological investigation!)

White Mykonos (1987)

A few years ago I had the good fortune to be marooned for several days in what was then the Mecca of jet-set gaydom. This is Mykonos, set like a jewel in the midst of the Aegean, and thought by some to be the most beautiful island in Greece.

You may well wonder how it was that a sedate Bostonian fag-of-letters should find himself in the international fast lane. I had planned to stay rather longer in Athens and then to spend a leisurely ten days island-hopping, stopping only briefly at Mykonos so as to visit the archaeological remains on nearby Delos. But the threat of a strike on the state ferries sent me to sea while I could at least get to Mykonos, though with no clear idea of how and when I might leave it.

Sleepless as Lady Macbeth during several days of combining rosy-fingered dawns with ambrosial nights in the noisy capital city, I was fleeing to the one Cycladic island which never sleeps. My guidebook listed no special festivals for Mykonos; instead, it read, "Life on Mykonos is one long festival." Not far wrong, I note in my diary, judging from the gilded youth of all nations who join the Greeks and the rest of us for the Sunday morning sailing of the *Panagia Tinoy*.

The ferry line admits to no firm schedule, since in the Aegean all ships arrive by the grace of Poseidon, but the best estimate is about seven hours. On the way out of Piraeus harbor, appropriately, we see the *Homerus* coming in. But on this day the sea is not wine-dark; rather, it is a beautiful royal blue, and our wake is turquoise. The taste of a stunningly sexy half-Greek, half-Italian, alcoholic "playboy" with whom I had had a brief but emotionally intense affair in Athens is stronger on my lips than the sea's salt breeze.

Mykonos town is an authentic island paradise. Approaching the harbor one sees first a clustering of what looks like sugar-cubes nestling along the esplanade. Once in port, one enters a honeycomb of eye-dazzling white buildings and whitewashed lanes, completely confusing in pattern. The near-universal whiteness is relieved by flowering shrubs, bright hanging textiles, wicker cages containing colorful birds, and expensive shops selling designer clothing, art works, icons, jewelry, or whatever. Mykonos has something like 350 shrine churches or chapels, some erected in thanksgiving for the proceeds of piracy. There is something appealingly earthy about that.

At sunset everyone goes to the outdoor cafés along the strand to drink wine or coffee or lemonade and watch the sunset; I gather that, for the real sophisticates, this is the equivalent of daybreak. Of course one can see why this island is such a haven for gays, and several are out and about at this time of evening. One bar, patronized by older gay men, is inviting in its decor. One listens to classical music while sitting on its terrace to watch Apollo Helios retire for the night.

After a morning's excursion to Delos by caïque, I return to the waterfront for lunch. Two French representatives of international fagdom are seated at the next table, waving their gold bracelets and having breakfast, which for them consists of bacon and eggs washed down with Coca-Cola. I see several European or American tourist/younger male Greek combinations, as well as more age-matched gay couples. It is not unprecedented to take someone over whom you're lost your head in Athens to Mykonos for a glamour vacation. My dark-eyed Athenian would willingly have come if asked, in spite of (or perhaps because of) a scheduled court appearance.

My *Spartacus* guidebook informs me that a year or so previously there had been a crackdown on gays enjoying al fresco sex in the little square in front of Paraportiani church. The normally tolerant islanders were not becoming puritanical about sex, on which the economic base of the island partly depends, but they did object (with good reason) to its venue. Partly because I am already suffering dehydration from the record-breaking heat of Athens, I do not investigate the famous nude gay beaches, such as "Super Paradise." These isolated spots were international drawing cards for gay men in the frantic 1970's and early 1980's; the boats ran late on moonlit nights, and the action in the dunes ran later still.

Instead, I content myself with people-watching and private exploration of Mykonos town, a marvelous mixture of Greek fishing port and St. Tropez. The fishermen work on their boats in the midst of the pelicans along the strand each day, and the craft are kept beautifully shined and painted, in stark contrast to the rust buckets of Provincetown. I have breakfast each morning at a sidewalk table nearly under my blue-shuttered bedroom window. A picture-postcard old farmer brings his vegetables to market each morning on a donkey, but the waiter arrives (at 7 A.M.) on a noisy moped. I break my fast with freshly squeezed orange juice, tea, and lightly toasted slices of delicious Greek bread, served with butter, jam and honey. Passing alongside my table in the first ten minutes are two working donkeys, an old lady with a sack of bread and onions, a run of sophisticates and travellers, an Orthodox priest carrying three lovely flowers, and a little boy with a water pistol.

For my evening meals I discover a restaurant which has been open only a week and therefore is largely patronized by islanders. But one mild and flower-fragrant night, as I sit at my table under a tree in the forecourt, I see half-a dozen young internationals of French and Belgian extraction having a convivial dinner prior to "le disco." As I savor my baby shrimps baked in tomato sauce, they raise their wine glasses, first with the English toast "Cheers!" and then, remembering, with its Greek equivalent," Yámas!" ("to your health!").

My denim-clad Athenian had taught me that phrase, over the pale Kephalonian wine we had shared at our nightly meals. "Bittersweet," I had told him then. And more so now, hearing it from these other lips, fortunate ones, not having lived long enough to understand the word "regret."

Should I have asked my dark-eyed Theseus, who had guided me through the labyrinth of my own mind, to come with me, to sound for a while the charms of the fast lane of Mykonos, in your basic but expensive sea, sand and sex vacation package? Now, when I remember white Mykonos, both the beauty and the pain come flooding back. And memories of seductive brown eyes and a body which would have delighted Praxiteles are with me still.

Yámas! But yes, also bittersweet.

Part Seven:
Making One's Own Gay History

Celebration (1974)

" I know nothing, except what everyone knows --
If there when Grace dances, I should dance."

With these lines from W. H Auden's "Whitsunday in Kirchstetten," Harvey Cox opens his "theological essay on festivity and fantasy," *The Feast of Fools*. Festivity, says Cox, is " the capacity for genuine revelry and joyous celebration," and fantasy is "the faculty for envisioning radically alternative life situations." As the concept of gay pride expands to suggest a renewal of the spirit as well as a brand of political activism, it seems appropriate to explore this notion of festivity in order to expand our consciousness of who we are as a people shortly to come together in celebration of Gay Pride Week.

"Only man celebrates," Cox reminds us. Festivity, distinctively marking our humanness, has three corollaries. One is excess: we intentionally "live it up" We alter our normal pattern of sleep, diet, spending, dress, private taboos. We drink "confusion to the wolf of want, damnation to dull care," and do things just for the ever-lovin' hell of it.

A second is "juxtaposition," or contrast. A holiday is exceptional, a realized alternative to routine. As such it makes us more self-aware, more critical of our daily round. Third, festivity is an act of affirmation. Celebration involves joy. It always says "yes" to life -- to a past event, to a future hope, or to our present condition despite pain and oppression.

"If it be granted that we say Yea to a single moment," wrote Frederick Nietzche, "then in so doing we have said Yea not only to ourselves, but to all existence." By the same token, the petty bickering, the sloppy reasoning, the childish ego-tripping, the "gayer-than-thou" attitudes which have made our annual gay pride parade controversies resemble a tempest in a chamberpot are effective ways of saying Nay to ourselves and to all existence. Can we pretend to be liberated and still deny the freedom to celebrate in his or her own way to any gay person whose life-style is not exactly the same as our own? Let each one of us search his or her own conscience for the answer.

To set up an inherent conflict between planning a "joyous parade" and planning a "political statement" is simply absurd. As festivity, a parade (like play, contemplation, and making love --Cox) is an end in itself. Yet this parade is also a political statement in that it demonstrates that gays need not always be invisible, need not forever conform to the expectations of the straight world, unless we so choose.

The notion that "things need not always be as they are" always has revolutionary implications, no matter how understated. In celebration we make affirmation of who we are at our most joyful, and thereby we outline the possibility of a fuller, richer life to come. With dotting the "i"s and crossing the "t"s of political correctness, celebration has nothing to do.

As for myself, I choose to dance with the children of grace, with those who say Yea to themselves and to all existence. And I summon my brothers and sisters to this week of celebration with Whitmanesque rhetorical excess:

> Light! light! faggots!
> Burst! dykes! burst!
> Out of your cages, lavender rhinos!
> Out of your grottoes, seers and soothsayers!
> Shine, shine, fireflies and butterflies!
> Join hands, world-changers and life-celebrators!
>
> Existence is a Divine comedy.
> Come play it with us, in laughter and in hope.

Out of the Closet and Into the Flicks (1974)

I knew it was going to be a bad trip when the phone rang in the middle of my afternoon nap. It was my editor, who said "Look, 'A Very Natural Thing' is opening in Boston on the 24th, and Jonathan's [the *Gay Community News* arts critic] been in Europe and we can't send him to New York to review it in advance. You saw it when you went down for the [Gay Pride] parade, so why don't you review it for us?"

I could think of several reasons, including incompetence, and I'd almost rather substitute for Joe Namath than for Jonathan Cross. But I did indeed dance along five miles of New York streets to the golden tones of Sheri Barden's electric bullhorn ("the sweetest music this side of liberation"), and I did go down by train the day before to conserve my aging bod for the ordeal and to see "A Very Natural Thing." I'm glad I went.

This first "post-liberationist" feature film is not a great film, but it is a good one. It is good because it is well made technically (some sound problems), beautifully photographed (in color), realistically conceived, telling in its use of domestic details, generally well acted, and more than ordinarily perceptive about human relationships in the gay world.

The story line is quite simple. David (Robert Joel) is an overly earnest young ex-monk who, having discovered he can't isolate his love of God from his love of men, leaves the monastery and finds a job as a teacher in New York City. He is picked up in a dance bar by a ruggedly handsome, self-centered Yale grad, Mark (Curt Gareth), a cynical bastard interested only in good looks and good sex. Pressured by David's confining and perhaps näive ideal of a long-term relationship based essentially on a heterosexual model, Mark starts straying, to David's great distress. For a while, they try other expedients: the Fire Island botanical garden, an arranged group sex episode, separate tricking and, after David splits, the baths.

David, wholly alone, watches the 1973 Christopher Street Gay Liberation Day parade from the sidewalk. This gives producer-director Christopher Larkin the opportunity to insert cameo shots of participants expressing their feelings about themselves and gay liberation, with marvelous propagandistic effect. In Washington Square David meets Jason (Bo White), a marcher. They talk, they go home to supper, and one thing leads to another.

Jason has been married and has a child; a short scene with his ex-wife (Deborah Trowbridge) is tender and loving. David has learned some things about human relationships by now, and when Jason asks him to move in, declines the marriage model in favor of a more autonomous but genuinely caring liaison with him. The picture ends "in process;" a new order of relationship is building. Indeed this is "a very natural thing," expressed metaphorically in a playful, vibrant nude run along the surf on a Truro beach.

Perhaps this scenario sounds too pat: pre-liberated sexual expression was bad; post-Stonewall, it's good. But this is merely a thread on which hang other levels of meaning and action. The film is episodic, and at one level it is a panorama, lovingly photographed, of New York and the range of the gay male scene therein. At another level, it is a highly sensual love story (rated "R"), but I don't think a reasonable person could call it pornographic. Nudity and indeed explicit sex are present, but never out of place or treated as ends in themselves.

The contrast between this and the alleged "artistic breakthrough" male feature length films of recent years such as "The Light From the Second Story Window" or "The Boys in the Sand" couldn't be more obvious. The mechanical sexual athletics of the latter group drive out all other values, including cinematic ones. In "A Very Natural Thing," the sexuality is merely an important part of a much larger value statement.

The film is equally far removed from "The Boys in the Band," which I saw in Boston a few days later. I left that film with a double Excedrin headache, product of my anger and frustration over the cruelty, the inhumanity of these alleged friends toward one another. The tension, the horrendousness of the stereotypes, and their probable widespread influence among the non-gay or indeed the gay public upset me greatly.

"The Boys" are not me, and they are not my friends. Larkin's film, by contrast, is about me, about my gay male friends, about your gay male friends, about real problems we face daily as we try to develop healthier, newer types of same-sex relationships. Without glossing over the rough spots, its great significance is that a film maker has finally dared to say with artistic and moral integrity, "Gay is indeed 'A Very Natural Thing.'"

Older gay men and women will not see this film without some inner risk, for it will again touch those tender scars with which we have covered the wounds of many years, and regrets over what might-have-been will make the experience bittersweet. Yet it is time we shed that scar tissue, and I found the film curiously therapeutic in this regard.

Younger gay women should see it, for although their struggle to be both woman and gay differs from the struggle of others to be both man and gay, we all need to understand as much as we can about how it feels to be the other. I hope it will be seen by a lot of straights, because it is such a positive affirmation of what it means to be gay and to love and to engage with the new and the unknown. But most of all this is a picture for young male gays to see and to ponder. As a constructive, emancipating, identity-forming experience, one could scarcely ask for more.

"A Very Natural Thing" is more than just another flick. It is more than just another gay flick. It is an event.

Some Infamous Gay Homophobes (1986)

The recent death from AIDS of New York attorney Roy Cohn dredged up a lot of memories for gay people of my generation. Roy Cohn began his meteoric rise to infamy nearly thirty-five years ago as chief investigator for U. S. Senator Joe McCarthy in the early 1950's. Although he went on to many other years of notoriety, he will primarily be remembered for that early association.

"McCarthyism" is commonly associated with hysterical anti-communism. But beginning in 1950 conservative politicians on the make, of whom McCarthy was only one, began publicly to associate "sexual perverts" with alleged Communist infiltration of the Federal government. There was a certain symmetry to the hue and cry. The Communists wanted the minds of average Americans, while the perverts were said to want their bodies. On the whole, the perverts would have had the better deal.

The hysteria, discussed in John D'Emilio's book *Sexual Politics, Sexual Communities*, looks ridiculous now, but certainly wasn't funny at the time. All through the 1950's there were witch hunts in civil government, the military, state and local communities, and industries with government contracts. Thousands of gays were excluded or fired from government-related jobs as a result. The FBI and the Post Office gathered data on gays, put tracers on their mail, and notified employers of their perverted tastes, causing gays in the private sector also to lose their jobs.

There were rumors at the time that Roy Cohn was homosexual, and that he and his co-investigator G. David Schine (who later married), and even McCarthy himself, were getting it on with each other, though some of this was radical fag-baiting. Until the end Cohn denied he was gay or had AIDS, but last summer he was being treated with an experimental anti-AIDS drug at the National Institutes of Health, allegedly after intervention by persons highly placed in the Reagan administration. Cohn had spent his life in the naked pursuit of power and the powerful, including leading Mafia figures, Aristotle Onassis, Barbara Walters, J. Edgar Hoover, Cardinal Spellman, Richard Nixon and Ronald Reagan, among others whom I would not invite to a dinner party. Just before his death he was disbarred by the New York Supreme Court. A sordid story, from start to finish.

At the time of Cohn's demise another infamous gay homophobe was trotting around the lecture circuit pimping his life story, in the appallingly mistitled book *The Gentleman From Maryland: The Conscience of a Conservative*. Former Representative Robert Bauman was an arrogant opponent of gay rights while in Congress, a champion of the Moral Majority and similar organizations, who got caught out picking up black teenagers at one of Washington's more dismal hustler bars by the very FBI surveillance he had supported in the case of others. His was an equally sordid tale, and even now that he's "out" and pleading for tolerance (which he isn't getting from his former associates), he still refuses to support gay rights legislation. In other words, he's peddling a book the brunt of which is to indicate how little he's learned from his experience.

For a long time there was an unwritten gay rule that you didn't disclose another gay person's orientation to any non-gay person under any circumstances. More recently the argument has been advanced that closeted gays who actively oppose gay rights measures should be publicly unmasked. In the debates over the ordination of homosexuals to the Episcopal priesthood a few years ago, a particularly obnoxious Texas bishop made vicious attacks on gays in the church until a gay priest, who had witnessed the good bishop's cavortings in the Club Baths on his frequent trips to New York, went to him privately and threatened to expose him to the Presiding Bishop unless he ceased his venom, which he did (at least in public.)

A better known example is that of John T. "Terry" Dolan, a founder and a executive director of the National Conservative Political Action Committee, a very powerful lobby which frequently supports rabid homophobes for Congress and opposes gay rights. Perry Deane Young, who had earlier co-authored Dave Kopay's coming-out story, wrote another book called *God's Bullies*, a study of the new religious right. In it he devoted several pages to Dolan's proclivities, including nocturnal visits to Washington's gay bars, and even interviewed one of Dolan's pickups to get the flavor of the experience. Public exposure in this case did not lead to the loss of Dolan's job, though he seems to have taken a lower profile afterwards.

Why the phenomenon of the homophobic gay? The usual defense is simple libertarianism. Dolan's argument, for instance, is that he is against gay rights because he is against civil rights legislation in general, as being too much government intervention. This of course flies in the face of a history of government intervention against gays which cannot be remedied except by positive legislation.

I think there is another reason, though, and that's fascination with power, which for some people (gay and straight) is an effective substitute for the free play of sexuality. There are some general insights into this relationship in a second-rate novel about the McCarthy era, Alexander Federoff's *The Side of the Angels* (1960). One of the characters, Warren Taggert, is an upper-class Clevelander who "comes out" sexually in New Orleans during Mardi Gras. As he couples with Mike Cowan, a wealthy and politically-connected Washingtonian, "A guttural shout tore through their chests and threw them, bound together, into insensible blackness." (I told you it was a second-rate novel!)

Warren moves to Washington, eventually breaks up with Mike, then goes to New York and gets involved with a right-wing, McCarthyite magazine, *American View*, which supports Gen. Douglas MacArthur for President in 1952. Says Federoff, "As forceful a motive as [Warren's] political conviction was his personal need. A secret outcast in his aberration [sic], he could in his work be associated with the most conformist of men.... Assuming conformity like a uniform, he turned his back forever on the loneliness of a homosexual's desperate existence."

Purple prose aside, there is an interesting insight here into Roy Cohn's behavior and that of others of his day and generation. Many of us had to choose between our sexuality and a "respectable" career, and in that sense between sexuality and personal power. A few went beyond that, on the power trip. The penalty for their lack of self-awareness and self-acceptance was borne, unfortunately, not by themselves but by other gay men and women. I know what the costs of that choice were and I hope I am not an unduly uncharitable person. But I have no more regret at Roy Cohn's death than I would have for the killing of a poisonous snake in my back yard.

NOTE (1989): On December 28, 1986, a month or so after this essay was first published, Terry Dolan died at age 36 of AIDS. The first news releases listed "the immediate cause of death" as "congestive heart failure." Dolan's brother Anthony, who was Ronald Reagan's chief speech writer, attacked the *Washington Post* for a later story revealing the AIDS aspect; Anthony also denies that his brother was gay. See Christopher Hitchens, "It Dare Not Speak Its Name: Fear and Self-Loathing on the Gay Right," in the August, 1987 *Harpers' Magazine* for a discussion of the relation of the gay right wing and the Reagan administration, including the Iran-Conta scandal. One of my former graduate students, a heterosexually married bisexual, was also the lover of a highly placed male Reagan administration official.

Playing With Words (1980)

It is spring in Boston, which means sunny, mild days alternating with raw and rainy ones. It also means window-box time for those of us who live in urban renovation neighborhoods, a type of ecological niche in which gays are often as numerous as pigeons.

A suburbanite friend has given us some wooden boxes which we have promptly bolted into place along our Victorian cast-iron fence, in order to avoid providing occasions of sin to those of our fallen brethren of the larcenous persuasion. This year, perhaps reflecting our gradually increasing self-disclosure, we have planted pansies, on the good old American business principle that it pays to advertise. The sight of them bravely flaunting their colors on this gloomy day sets us to ruminating about the delights of what Bruce Rodgers has called *The Queen's Vernacular* (whose publisher is Straight Arrow, no less).

One of the special benefits of having a gay vernacular is that sheer delight which comes when one gleefully and wilfully misreads a key word or phrase. Something more or less sensible in conventional terms often makes a special in-crowd double entendre when heard by gay ears (or seen by gay eyes, for that matter). Thus the sight of 1939 history of American wags and eccentrics entitled *Grandfather Was Queer* raises fascinating questions about the old gentleman's sexual orientation; is it possible that Foxy Grandpa had a lover on the side? A couple of month ago, while browsing in Goodpeed's bookshop, I encountered a book of short stories published in 1930 entitled *Gay Agony*, by one H. A. Manhood. Nothing extraordinary about the content, but think of the possibilities!

A couple of years ago the Sheraton people built a motel just off the Massachusetts Turnpike, after the manner of an Irish castle. In front is one of those signs which can be set to flash various messages. In accordance with the feudal motif of the building, one of the early programs included "Be a Queen for a Knight." A young gay friend to whom I told this tale insisted that I was pulling his leg, which I should certainly like to have done, but my credibility was restored when I drove him past and he saw it for himself. Alas, someone must have tipped off the management, for that message has been dropped from the repertoire, though now whenever I pass the motel the mental image returns.

The most recent, and perhaps most spectacular gaffe (if it is that) along these lines has been perpetrated by a presumably unsuspecting General Mills, Inc. Greeting me from the shelves of my local super market a few weeks back was a new kind of breakfast cereal called "Body Buddies," which I promptly bought." "Body Buddies" come (or comes) in two flavors, "natural fruit" and "brown sugar and honey," a choice which ought to satisfy everyone's taste in body buddies. (I prefer the sugar/honey type to the au naturel variety, which perhaps tells you that I am just another one of your run-of-the-mine traditional effete Eastern perverts and not one of the newer macho Western types.)

In addition to the cereal, the package contains the admonition that "a good breakfast [is one] consisting of juice, toast, milk, and of course, Body Buddies!" Each box also contains a "Body Buddies' Fun Book" which, though not up to *The Joy of Gay Sex*, is "filled with games, tricks, puzzles and jokes you can do with friends or by yourself." (I assume these statements need no scholarly glosses.) The rebus on my brown sugar and honey box works out to "I promise to do my homework every night." The natural fruit box offers a personalized cereal spoon for which you send in, not three box tops, but rather three body buddies box bottoms! (Try saying that quickly.)

The cereal isn't half bad, but as you can see I really get my jollies from the packaging. One wonders whether gay consciousness has not yet penetrated the Minneapolis headquarters of General Mills or, alternatively, whether it has. This could be a giant, nation-wide hoax put on by some three-piece-suited, subversively inclined closeted gay wordsmith in the promotion department with a finely honed sense of just what can and cannot be gotten past the Board of Directors. If so, this could be the most effective form of positive gay advertising since Sgt. Leonard Matlovitch in his true-blue air force uniform hit every corner drugstore in America via a *Time* magazine cover.

One sign of being comfortable with one's gayness, I think, is the ability to take words that may once have hurt us and, by using them in a playful fashion, defuse and defang them for others. This doesn't always work. Back in the early days of the *Gay Community News* (late 1973, I think), our perceptive theatre critic used the word "faggot" in this wise. One super-uptight patron wrote in angrily cancelling his subscription, faulting the editor for having allowed one of his columnists to use that word! But I'm all in favor of making in-house jokes and *Christopher Street*-type cartoons and being relaxed about our collective foibles, expressions and practices. I think that this kind of mucking around with words really builds us a sort of backfire against the flames of the hostiles.

In that spirit, it seems to me that the new General Mills venture suggests a solution to a long-standing gay word problem, which is what to call the other member of your binary same-sex household. "Friend," "roommate," "companion," and, more recently "lover" have all been tried and, at least by some, found wanting. Though "lover" is a word I find perfectly useful, writers of etiquette books stumble over the problem, agonized parents don't know how to refer to their son's or daughter's "Um...," and so forth. My GCN counterpart, columnist and poet Nancy Walker, has taken the sociopsychological term "significant other" and shortened it to "sother" as a special term for the woman with whom she shares her life, but seems to have found no imitators.

Now that General Mills has captured the public's attention with its nationally distributed new breakfast cereals, however, let me suggest that gays adopt the term "body buddy" as a synonym for "lover." It's reasonably brief, rather catchy, sensuous without being salacious. Altogether a happy solution, I should say.

Besides, gays since Socrates have been accused of corrupting youth, but the best-kept secret of the gay movement is that we don't really do a very effective job of it. If modern theories of psychogenesis have any validity, it's the heterosexual family unit which mass-produces gay youth out of polymorphously perverse pansexual infants. Why should we then not publicly admit defeat and let good old American corporate and advertising know-how have a crack at doing our corrupting for us? Surely a generation of healthy Americans conditioned through their morning cereal boxes to the value of having body buddies can't grow up all bad!

NOTE (1989): General Mills evidently overestimated the gay breakfast food market; perhaps no one told them that nowadays self-respecting gays only do brunch. In any event, "Body Buddies" disappeared from the shelves of my super market in less than a year. Too bad. First thing in the morning I'd rather face a cereal box with a handsome hunk playfully glancing back at me than a puritanical warning that my cholesterol count will go through the roof if I don't consume my daily quota of oat bran.

Anita Redux (1981)

NOTE (1989): In January, 1977 the Dade County (Florida) Commission enacted an ordinance protecting the civil rights of gays in housing, public accommodations, and employment. A successful fight to repeal the ordinance by referendum was led by Anita Bryant, a pop singer and former Miss America runner-up whose marriage and career were both in decline, and who was currently making television commercials for Florida orange juice. A gay boycott of Florida orange juice followed, and the consumption level of screwdrivers in gay bars dropped substantially. Demonstrations against Bryant, led by angry gays, were held in many cities (including Boston) in which she later had singing or speaking engagements; Bryant complained vociferously that gays had ruined her singing career.

She subsequently separated from her husband and moved to Alabama to open a dress shop, at which point she gave the long interview to the *Ladies' Home Journal* discussed below, initially misreported in the Boston and the national press. The Rev. Dr. Endicott Newbury Boylston is a fictional creation; "Newbury" and "Boylston" are Back Bay streets much frequented by gay Bostonians. The dialogue reflects my own ambivalence about our gay movement leadership, whose qualities of heart I admire rather more than I sometimes do their qualities of judgement. Surely the skies are not always falling.

The other night I passed a quiet evening in the Back Bay home of that excessively cultivated Anglican divine, the Rev. Dr. Endicott Newbury Boylston, sometime rector of St. Swithin's Parish and Honorary Canon of the Cathedral of St. Botolph. Fr. Boylston is one of the last leaves of an ancient family tree rooted firmly in the soil of colonial Boston.

Early on the Boylstons were members of the Mathers' Second Church, but like nearly all of Boston's leading families they shifted to Unitarianism early in the nineteenth century. Cottie's own branch, however, had become High Church Episcopalians after the Civil War, and to the great scandal of his Unitarian relatives a great-uncle had followed Father Huntington into the Order of the Holy Cross. Cottie himself has been at odds for a full three generations now with those to whom he is wont to refer, in his more charitable moments, as "the low-church prelates of this misguided Diocese."

After dining on Cornish game hen and honeydew we adjourned to the library, where I admired his latest acquisition, an early nineteenth century plaster copy of the Marble Faun once owned by Nathaniel Hawthorne. "Posed just like any young hustler in Park Square, isn't he?" Cottie remarked gleefully. The room was in more than its usual state of disorder, since the good doctor had been discreetly weeding the private files of a deceased fellow cleric of similar tastes and interests, as the last stage in what is locally called "setting one's affairs." ("Alas," quoth Cottie, "some of his affairs will never be settled!") As we sipped our brandy, I noticed a copy of the December, 1980 *Ladies' Home Journal* next to his chair. "Aren't you being a bit obvious?," I snickered.

"My boy," he replied (to Cottie, any male under the age of seventy is "my boy"; he and the century were in their teens together), "we'll have none of the tacky inanities with which you regale your miniscule coterie of quasi-literate readers. It is incumbent on any responsible presbyter occasionally to plumb the shallows of the American religious mind, especially in these days of the 'born-again Christian'. The local press was so excited about Anita Bryant's alleged coming out as a 'reborn born-againner' that I had to secure the original interview in this magazine. Unfortunately, like drinking decaffeinated coffee or kissing one's sister, the anticipation was more titillating than the result."

"Do you mean she hasn't repented of her sins against gays?" I asked, incredulous. "Why, the headline in the *Boston Globe* claimed 'Bryant Says She Has Changed, Believes in Live and Let Live'."

"My boy," he replied, "you ought to know that since the *Transcript* ceased publication in 1941 there hasn't been a newspaper in Boston on which an intelligent person can rely. No, she hasn't 'repented of her sins' as you so Evangelically put it. She does indeed say 'live and let live,' but she follows that by 'just don't flaunt it or try to legalize it.'

"As for the rest of the interview, it's hardly worthy of Page One when a popular entertainer of extraordinarily limited background and talent finally realize that 'fundamentalists have their heads in the sand'; some of us have been saying that for decades. Don't you recall the old saw about Anglicanism being the point of balance between 'the meretricious gaudiness of the Church of Rome and the squalid sluttery of a fanatical conventicle'? The real problem lay in your activist friends taking this poor, ignorant, Valium-popping walking media event seriously."

"Now wait a minute, Cottie," I exclaimed. "I'm tempted to agree with you about Anita per se. I felt at the time that a lot of gay activists lost their heads over her rantings with a speed suggesting that those selfsame heads weren't screwed on very tightly in the first place. But there is a larger phenomenon out there: the Moral Majority, Jerry Falwell, electronic evangelism and all the rest of it. You may regard them as Yahoos, but they're out organizing against us, even among some elements of the Episcopal church."

"My boy," he replied, "Episcopalians may be retrograde, theologically and socially; probably most of them are. But please bear in mind that it is canonically impossible, even in these degenerate days, to be an Episcopalian and a Yahoo at one and the same time.

"In any case, Bryant isn't the first Yahoo I've seen self-destruct, and she won't be the last. Years ago I covered the Scopes trial for the *Anglo-Catholic Gazette* and witnessed the self-destruction of William Jennings Bryan. And it was in this very room, over a glass of my grandfather Hallowell's best port, that Joe Welch and I planned the strategy leading to the self-destruction of Senator "Tail-Gunner Joe" McCarthy. You'll recall Ben Franklin's astute observation, at the age of sixteen, in one of his Silence Dogood essays: "An indiscreet Zeal for spreading an Opinion, hurts the cause of the Zealot". That's something some of your activist friends might take to heart, as well."

I took a few moments to skim the Bryant interview, especially the sections concerning gays, which Cottie had marked. "You're right," I said. "On the one hand she says that the church needs to love gays as human beings, unconditionally, yet she follows that immediately by saying that "If I had it to do over, I'd do it again, but not in the same way.' It looks as though the real 'tortured turnabout,' as the *Journal* has it, was a pretty self-interested one. She's shifted a bit on the divorce issue and on male supremacy in the household, and that's about it."

"Well, all of that is so much leather and prunella," Cottie snapped. "Those who live by the media will die by the media. The point is, if you'd lived as long as I, you'd realize that the Yahoos have always been with us, and that periodically they go on the rampage; that's what democracy's all about. But I've never felt compelled to roll over and play dead when it happens."

"Cottie," I said, "you're one of a dying breed. We're now into the five R's: Reagan, reaction, retrenchment, repentance, and rearmament. The most strenuous form of physical exercise in certain liberal quarters nowadays is throwing in the towel. But let's suppose you were in a position to address a group of gay activists. What counsel would you have for them?""

"My boy," he replied, "supposing I were to be caught in that compromising position, my first piece of advice would be to cultivate some historical perspective, beginning with young Boswell's excellent new treatise on *Christianity, Social Tolerance and Homosexuality.* Then I should advise them that minority success in our society has always rested on four things: keeping your head when those around you are losing theirs, developing support networks, choosing your battlegrounds carefully, and then girding up your loins with the truth within you. That may all sound as old-fashioned as my grandmother's spring bonnet, but it has worked before and it will work again."

I left my aged friend to his archival labors and walked home across the moonlit city. Here is the snow-clad Episcopal church where Integrity/ Boston is welcomed each week; there a restaurant where a gay man was recently shot to death and his lover wounded; down the street is a recently opened gay disco. Yonder are three shivering teenaged hustlers in search of a warm bed and some bread. Beyond them is a neighborhood of old brick houses lovingly restored by gay hands.

It's still a pretty mixed bag for gays, I thought as I turned my key in the lock, reflecting on the diversity of gay need and gay accomplishment I'd encountered in a few short blocks. Yet Cottie's words washed over me:

"I've never felt compelled to roll over and play dead... gird up your loins with the truth within you... it has worked before and it will work again." Cottie's is a fighting faith; may it be so for my generation, and for gay generations to come.

Of STD's and Magic Bullets (1986)

The AIDS crisis has forced us as a people to confront the issues of causality, spread, duration and control which every mysterious epidemic in history has posed to those caught up in it. To the extent that disease can be understood as more than a medical phenomenon, we can begin to use its history to illuminate our present dilemmas and, one hopes, to blunt the scape-goating and moral misconstructions which frequently follow in its wake.

I recommend Allen Brandt's 1985 book *No Magic Bullet: A Social History of Venereal Disease in the United States Since 1880* to any gay person seriously concerned about an "AIDS backlash" as the level of public panic continues to rise. Some medical historians used to refer to the twentieth century as the era of "the conquest of epidemic disease." Yet, as Brandt shows, the sexually transmitted diseases (STD's) provide a unique subset of the infectious diseases in that they are either inadequately controlled or out of control.

When I was young, my parents worried about such child health matters as the annual summer polio outbreaks. My sisters and I brought home whooping cough, chickenpox, measles and mumps from school as one would homework, as a matter of course. As an adolescent, I nearly died of pneumonia. Most of these ailments are now considered relatively minor public health problems.

As a young man, the only two STD's I ever heard about were syphilis and gonorrhea. Since those innocent days, about thirty others appear to have been invented, several of them now worldwide, or pandemic. And whoever would have thought, in my salad days, that a grasp of the technology of the condom would become de rigeur for gay males in rut?

Our society's inability to eradicate the STD's, Brandt argues, is rooted in a two-fold misconception. On the one hand, we cling to a concept of disease as a departure from some ideal biological norm, to be "cured" by a biotechnological fix, after which we would all live happily ever after, tra la, tra la. On the other, when it comes to the STD's, we strangely change the model by over-loading these inconvenient micro-organisms with images of corruption, vice, pollution, uncleanness, a decaying social order and God's or Nature's punishment for sexual or moral laxity.

These two beliefs have exercised a powerful influence both on medical practice and on public policy. For example, Brandt tells of the great opposition from social hygienists to the issuance of prophylactic kits for American soldiers in France during World War I, on the grounds that the soldier unpatriotic enough to expose himself to VD deserved to suffer the consequences. The practical result was that VD was second only to the influenza epidemic as a scourge of the troopers by the end of the war.

Twice in this century "magic bullets" against the STD's have been proclaimed. The first was Paul Ehrlich's discovery of Salvarsan as a VD "cure" in 1909. The second was mass production of penicillin during World War II, as much in demand for military VD control as for controlling the effects of wounds. In 1938 the Congress had passed the National Venereal Disease Control Act, providing federal funding for VD clinics, diagnostic facilities, and medical treatment for the indigent. But the Public Health Service proved unable to get the general or the medical public to rethink the STD's as just another set of infectious diseases.

Nevertheless, by the mid 1950's, VD rates had been brought down to an all-time low in the U.S. Ironically, as a result, people began to get careless again. The apparatus for dealing with the problem was gradually dismantled through cuts in Federal and state funding, closing facilities, and less training of specialists in what seemed to be an ailment without a future. Predecessors of the Moral Majority stimulated public opposition to funding for VD control, on the grounds that if sex became safe, promiscuity would reign and American society fall apart. Brandt argues that the rapid rise in the STD's since 1958 is not primarily due to the "sexual revolution" of the 'sixties, but rather to such ill-advised budget-cutting, and the unforeseen consequences thereof.

Brandt brings his story down to the current herpes and AIDS epidemics, showing how they both reflect and are caught up in social attitudes which have clustered around the STD's for a full century. The notion that VD is a disease of the "other," of people who have sinned or been bad people or however we want to divide the "them" from the "us," permeates the public response to AIDS. It may even be found, I regret to discover, in the condescending attitudes which some gay men have shown toward other gay men afflicted with AIDS or ARC. Caught up in our unstated and unchallenged received assumptions about STD's, we trap ourselves and our fellow human beings in a cycle of guilt, blame and alienation which we lack the wit and the historical wisdom to break.

We are as yet only toddlers on the shore of the great sea of ignorance which it will be necessary to breast before understanding the cause, course and cure of AIDS. We cannot afford to be misled by promises of magic bullets, by the unthinking repetition of centuries-old social attitudes, and by lack of appreciation of the ways in which disease is socially constructed.

The history of public health may offer further ammunition to combat the tired arguments of those who would use the AIDS crisis as one more weapon in the social enforcement of bigotry and hatred. When a mayoral candidate in Houston (fortunately defeated) proclaims that the best way of solving the AIDS problem is to "shoot the queers," he and others like him need to be forcibly reminded that, even in the era of no magic bullets, nowadays the queers are prepared to shoot back.

Samaritans All (1986)

The recent expeditions by Dr. Robert Ballard and associates at the Woods Hole Oceanographic Institution for the propose of discovering and photographically exploring the RMS *Titanic* have focused public attention on the great age of luxury steamship travel before World War I.

The loss of the *Titanic* was perceived either as a tragic "freak of nature" or "act of God," depending on how one looks at the world. But soon afterwards came the destruction of a number of other great ocean liners, this time by the hand of man, during the German submarine blockade of Britain and France in the early part of the war. The most famous of these was the Cunarder RMS *Lusitania*, sunk off Ireland with great loss of life on May 7, 1915.

In Boston's Back Bay there is a memorial to two of the victims of the *Lusitania* sinking, a structure which gay men and women have come to know well in the last couple of years. The Leslie Lindsey Memorial Chapel, constructed in 1924, is dedicated to the memory of a young Boston woman and her English-born husband, who together lost their lives in that tragic demonstration of human destructiveness.

Emmanuel Church, the Episcopal ecumenical center to which the Lindsey Chapel is attached, was constructed during another great American tragedy, the Civil War. When I first attended services there, the ushers wore cutaways and the ladies white gloves, but those days are long past. Emmanuel Church is now perhaps best known as the only church in the world which regularly performs the full cycle of Bach's 200 sacred cantatas in the context of the Sunday morning liturgy. But the parish also has a history of social outreach and spiritual healing, expressed in Lesley Lindsey's day by its settlement house and in the Emmanuel Movement. The latter was an early attempt to link spiritual resources and physical health concerns. Emmanuel's example informed the approach to healing taken by the founders of Alcoholics Anonymous in the 1930's.

Emmanuel Church opened its doors to organized gay concerns several years ago when it gave meeting space to Integrity/Boston and helped host the 1980 Integrity national convention. More recently, it has several times made the Lindsey Chapel available to the AIDS Action Committee and the AIDS Interfaith Coalition for healing services. All too many times also, it has been used for memorial services to commemorate the lives of our brothers who have died of AIDS.

The English Gothic chapel is long, high and narrow, for it was built on the site of a single Back Bay town house. One walks off Newbury Street into a dark vestibule, then into the light of a stunning nave forty-six feet high and eighty-five feet long. Behind the simple altar is an elaborate reredos. On the reredos are thirty-five alabaster female saints (and a niche for another, stolen several years ago), as well as one of Mary and her mother St. Anne, and one of St. Elizabeth and her son St. John the Baptist. In the center is a youthful, androgynous representation of the risen Christ. Suddenly one is taken with the feminist symbolism, even to the dominant blue (a color traditionally associated with Mary) of the stained glass windows.

Lindsey Chapel is a place where we are creating our history as gay men and women in a time of great crisis. We have gone there to celebrate the lives and mourn the deaths of many we know, or perhaps did not know. We have prayed there for healing, for compassion, for solidarity, and sometimes for release. Even those who are not of the faith celebrated in the Chapel are comforted by the healing beauty and symbolic richness of the space, by the sound of our collective voices and of beautiful music echoing back to us from walls and ceiling, and by the simple presence of each other. In it we have broken through to a further understanding of our own mortality, but also to a fuller realization of our common humanity.

Bach's Cantata 164, "You Who Call Yourselves Christians," recalls the story of the Good Samaritan, who stopped to care for a stranger who had been robbed and beaten. "Samaritan hearts let the stranger's pain hurt them," sings the alto, "and they are rich in goodness and mercy."

Yet the tale is so familiar that we miss its significance. Like us, Samaritans were a despised people, a mixed lot not "pure" enough for the mainstream culture of their day and place. The orthodox, the priest and the Levite, crossed the road to avoid getting involved with the stranger lying half-dead by the roadside. "They act as if they know nothing of the stranger's suffering," the bass soloist tells us. "They pour neither wine nor oil on their neighbor's wounds."

The essence of the story is distilled in a line Bach gives to the tenor soloist. The Samaritan test, if one may call it that, is to love compassionately, so that "the distress of my neighbor, no matter who he is, friend or foe, pagan or Christian, *shall touch my heart as my own suffering*" (emphasis mine). I don't think many of us can meet that test fully. We say "why me?" or "Why us?" or "I can't deal with that right now" or "It's all too depressing" or, if a child of the sixties, "that's not my bag."

But of course at this point in our history it is our bag, and we have to deal with its contents of fear, hatred, suffering and death. I think about that a lot as I listen to those wonderful Bach cantatas, or when I take my place in Lindsey Chapel or elsewhere among those who mourn. And I think about the Samaritan ethic when I see the best of a whole generation of gay men who, knowing that they themselves may well be (as they put it) "walking time-bombs," have nevertheless put self and fear aside and thrown themselves into the fight against AIDS, or into the nurture of its casualties.

In another of Bach's cantatas there is a delightful image of "the sheep no one would steal." Some of us can identify with that! If there is anything of worth to be distilled out of this terrible scourge, it is that we are learning to value our diverse selves and to discover in adversity the truth of a phrase which has stuck in my mind ever since reading it in Howard Brown's *Familiar Faces, Hidden Lives*. It is this: "What is important and of abiding moral concern is how fully and generously a person lives his life."

Part Eight:
Two Days, A Seemingly Fictional Memoir

PREFATORY NOTE (1989):

In January, 1980, Felice Picano wrote to ask me to attempt an unfamiliar genre, the short story, for consideration in an anthology of new gay fiction, poetry and drama he was then commissioning and editing. The volume was intended to reflect the range and diversity of American gay life, and Felice wanted to include something from an observer of long-term change. This might be an essay, but ideally it would be a fictional piece "showing the problems of communication between older and younger gays."

My first reaction, which I probably should have heeded, was "the shoemaker should stick to his last." But after thinking about it, I decided to go ahead and try a fictional piece. Six months later I produced a first draft. It was clear both to Felice and to me, however, that it did not work as a short story, though a piece or two, blown up, might. Conversely, it might serve as an abstract for a longer fictional piece, perhaps even the Great American Gay Novel. (Move over, Andrew Holleran!)

I have picked it up two or three times since 1980 and monkeyed with the text here and there, but of course it still doesn't work as a short story, for a variety of reasons. I include it here, however, because I think it does more or less work in the context of my other writing, essentially as a long retrospective quasi-fictional essay, packed with remembered detail which must either be set down or be lost. Sometimes ideas work out a little more easily when they can be explored with the techniques of fiction, as in "Anita Redux" earlier in this book. I was myself surprised, in reading it over as I thought about what to include in this volume, to discover how "Two Days" seemed to tie up and explain, even to me, many of the values, ideas and positions I had tried to convey, implicitly or explicitly, in my essays.

The purpose of the "memoir" was to evoke reflection both on continuity and change in the gay world and on the now-vanished world of civility, grace, and cultural ferment I knew in Manhattan in the mid-fifties. Surnames, given names, biographical data, and some incidents are drawn from my mother's family and from my own experiences, but I have scrambled them in many cases to simplify and otherwise fit the story.

Thus while the detail is sometimes fictionalized, it is rooted in autobiographical fact, at least in part, and therefore expresses certain truths of American urban social history. Large landowning families like my mother's on Long Island did intermarry with other English and Dutch proprietary families in the seventeenth and eighteenth centuries. Many moved to Manhattan in the nineteenth century and became brokers, patrons of culture, and Episcopalians. In the post World War I period (and sometimes earlier) they fled to the suburbs, leaving behind their single and gay members. These, in turn, along with Jewish and gay intellectuals coming to New York from very different local origins, were responsible for the cultural efflorescence of New York in the 1950's. At the same time, there was a new immigration of southern and Caribbean blacks and of Hispanics from Cuba and Puerto Rico, who were so dramatically to change the complexion of Manhattan in succeeding years.

Much of the sex is, alas, fictional; no doubt the product of an overwrought imagination acting on a lack of opportunity. (I am reminded of James McNeill Whistler's famous reflection on his less than rewarding year at West Point: "Had silicon been a gas, I would have been a major general.") But I make no apology for wishing the Lenox collection into existence; some years ago I was involved in an unsuccessful attempt to establish a gay archives and book collection at New York Public's 42nd Street Research Library, which was founded in part on an earlier Lenox Library of rare books, manuscripts, and works of art housed in a building on the present site of the Frick Museum.

Finally, I have rejected the notion that gays were invented with disco or Stonewall or the urban-industrial revolution. While fully recognizing that changing culture conditions the expression of sexual variance, implicit in most of my essays and explicit in this one is a more irenic position which affirms linkages with all that sexually variant men and women have thought, done, produced, or created throughout all the corridors of human time. Some of our gay illuminati dissent fiercely from that proposition, and of course they are perfectly free to do so. For my own part, however, I do not care for a priori restrictions on inquiry into the lives of sexually variant men and women who have the gay and human potential to become "some of my best friends."

Two Days (1980)

He shook his head, like a spaniel emerging from an unexpected rain shower, and the world took form again. The raucous urban sounds filtering into his bedroom mingled incongruously with the fragment of classical music with which his brief dream had ended. The warm lump along his leg, whose weight had given him an awakening cramp, meowed and bit his ankle in protest against his movements. It was nearly five. I must be getting older, he thought, to sleep almost two hours on a Saturday afternoon.

He moved slowly to the kitchen, fed the disgruntled cat, and remembered that he was due at the Blydenburghs at seven for drinks and dinner. Ted Blydenburgh was his second cousin and oldest friend; they had roomed together in college. His wife was a cheery, talented woman who had always managed to stand out independently of Ted's accomplishments, combining family life with a career in interior design.

It will probably be a typical East Side party, he though sardonically. Ted's medical associates would be symbolically clutching their Reagan buttons while watching an argument among local reform Democrats of both genders over whether Richard Nixon should or should not have been zoned out of the neighborhood. The now fading "Philadelphia blondes," the Grace Kelly-like feminine ideal of his youth, would grow tipsy on Chivas Regal while quietly boasting of their children's graduations, engagements, weddings and assorted liaisons. Fifties debutantes were almost the last people he knew, except gay ribbon clerks, who still drank Scotch. There would be, no doubt, the usual half-dozen carefully coiffed upper East Side queens from among Elaine's professional associates. Oh, well, he thought, his grandmother had instilled in him the notion that accepted invitations are implied obligations. If necessary, he could take advantage of his recent hospitalization to make his farewells early and be home by eleven.

As he shaved and dressed, he wondered what his grandmother would have thought of this kind of social mixture. She had been born on the upper East Side a hundred years ago next November. Her own mother had been born in 1855 in an elegant town house still standing along Colonnade Row. He recalled attending a rather decadent party there about a century later in the apartment on the parlor floor, where he had "made out" with a Marine corporal on the Swedish modern sofa incongruously blocking the marble mantel.

His grandparents had kindled in him a life-long fascination with this battered city, though by the 1930's they had sold the spacious Queen Anne on Staten Island, from which his grandfather had commuted by ferry to his office at the foot of Broadway, and had taken refuge in a Bronxville apartment. As a child, his parents existed for him primarily in a few photographs and fading newspaper accounts recording his mother's engagement and marriage to a brash stunt-flying broker, and his father's rumored suicide in the crash of his private plane in November, 1929, shortly after the collapse of his six-month-old firm. His own birth the following May had been overshadowed by his mother's death from a hospital infection; she had been the first of her line not to have her baby at home.

In the fifties he had puzzled his contemporaries by spending so much of his time with older men. Gay men of those days, who looked to Freudian-influenced developmental psychology to understand themselves, charged him with searching for a "father figure." It wasn't that simple, he thought irritably. The real problem for a young gay person, then and now, was how to link up with people like his grandparents, people who had known who and what they were and acted out of that self-knowledge, coupled with a sense of responsibility for the care and nurture of others.

During his childhood and adolescence his grandparents and his granmother's older sister, Aunt Susan, had shared with him the things in which they were interested. His grandfather's avocation was mineralogy, which had led him to a life-long concern with science education and eventually to the Vice-Presidency of the New York Mineralogical Society. His grandmother's genealogical intersts took her and the boy through the old residential streets of lower Manhattan and Brooklyn (not yet invaded by "Brownstoners"), seeking out venerable residential areas, forgotten churches, and the waterfront sites associated with the maritime interests of her husband's family. From his Aunt Susan, an artist who was for many years an executive with the Humane Society, he caught not only a late-Victorian sense of responsibility for all living things but also an interest in theatre, music and painting. (Unlike many men of his class and sexual orientation, however, he never managed to master the special language of ballet.) As he adjusted his narrow 1950's necktie and prepared to go downstairs to meet his taxicab, he wondered idly for the thousandth time whether his great-aunt had been a lesbian, and concluded for the five-hundredth that the anwer was "probably not." Susan's engagement to a twenty-three year old cousin had been unexpectedly and painfully broken by his death from typhoid while a volunteer with Teddy Roosevelt's Rough Riders in '98. Had it been social control or psychological self-discovery which had led her to renounce marriage thereafter? He supposed he'd never know.

· · · · ·

The cat, coming alive with the sunbeams on a perfect Sunday morning, woke him again at 6:45. While the coffee brewed, he relaxed in his favorite chair and thought about the previous evening. As usually, the party hadn't been half so bad in actuality as it had been in anticipation. In fact, he'd rather enjoyed it; Elaine was the best hostess he knew. Ted, who like himself was one of that vanishing breed, an old-line liberal Republican, had scared up not only a former Mayor of New York of that persuasion but a couple of staff writers from the heyday of the *New York Herald Tribune* (which his grandfather had always called "The Herald"). They had reminisced about the days when it was pre-eminently a writer's paper, with the likes of Walter Lippman, Walter Terry, Eugenia Sheppard, Clementine Padelford, John Crosby, the Alsops and Virgil Thomson making regular contibutions in a style an educated person could read without a shudder, in contrast to the turgid, self-righteous prose of the *New York Times*. He'd also gotten into an interesting conversation with a middle-aged woman who as a recent Barnard graduate had done volunteer work with his grandmother, and now was using her college language skills as a counselor at a home for single mothers, many of whom spoke little English.

Also present had been a gay liberationist playwright with whom he had debated the value of "message" drama. He had been delighted to discover that his new acquaintance could discuss the work of Maxwell Anderson, T. S. Eliot, Tennessee Williams, and other fifties theatrical luminaries with far more balance, precision and insight than he had been able to muster in drawing from his memories of attendance at their plays. No question, he mused, that in spite of the tiresomeness of some of the gay "movement" types he'd had the misfortune to encounter, there were signs of promise in all this ferment, perhaps especially in the arts.

He smiled as he recalled a line from one of his childhood's favorite romances, Rafael Sabatini's *Scaramouche*. In that book, the young revolutionary-artist-hero had rationalized his impromptu acting career by saying "In my humble way I am a student of man, and some years ago I made the discovery that he is most intimately to be studied in the reflections of him provided for the theatre." And, congratulating himself on the wildly promiscuous memory which could regularly dredge up lines like this, he absentmindedly burnt his fingers while getting an English muffin out of the toaster.

• • • • •

It was Sunday afternoon, the kind of mild, fresh late-spring weather one gets in the city before summer's Bermuda High closes in. Although during the winter he usually attended services nearer home, as the weather moderated he always enjoyed exploring one or another of the numerous Episcopal churches (now often dwindling in attendance, and much neglected) designed by Richard Upjohn, Minard LaFever and others from the high season of Victorian Gothic: Holy Communion on 6th Avenue, St Peter's in

Chelsea, lich-gated Transfiguration on 29th, and so many others. This Sunday, however, he had chosen to attend services at the Cathedral, where as a graduate student at Columbia in the middle 'fifties he had been regularly drawn, in part by the theologically and socially relevant preaching of Dean James Pike and in part by the Chapter's efforts to reach out to all manner of folk in the neighborhood. It was a path which had taken a later Bishop of New York, whose mother had been a friend of his great-aunt's, to the point of ordaining an open lesbian priest in another forgotten little Episcopal parish church, LaFever's Italianate Church of the Holy Apostles on the west side of mid-town, in 1977. He had wholeheartedly supported that decision, as he had supported the ordination of women generally, in opposition to the views of his own Rector and a majority of his home parish.

He had not always been faithful to the church of his mother's family, however. Only in his forties had he begun to reconsider his relationship to the institutional church. He and his cousin had flirted with Quakerism at Swarthmore, just as they had flirted with sex with each other on early adolescent overnight visits. Neither experiment had taken with Ted, who was Dutch Reformed by birth and agnostic by temperament, and only the homosexuality had persisted with himself. His vestryman grandfather had died during the spring vacation of his freshman year, and his grandmother early in 1954, just as he was completing a two-year hitch with the Army in Japan, during the last phases of the Korean War.

When he came back to the States in June he was restless, like any number of Korean vets. He was also depressed over the death of his grandmother and by Aunt Susan's apparent decline, though she was still good company on the occasional theatre or museum expedition. A few weeks before she died they had seen Orson Welles, who had sprained one ankle at rehearsal and the other at an early performance, do "King Lear" at the City Center from a gleaming modern wheelchair; such was the bravura nature of the production that he had not found it incongruous.

He had bought time for a year by filling in as a teacher of classics and history in a New England preparatory school. But it became clear to him, at this stage of his life, that he could not handle the constant contact with sexually overcharged teen-aged males in the classroom, on the athletic field, and above all running half-naked around the residence of which he was nominally master. A tense year finished without incident and he went back to Manhattan, enrolling at Columbia under the G.I. Bill to study for an M.A. in the humanities, for no better reason than that it seemed like an interesting program and would give him more time to sort things out.

• • • • •

Blinking like a lost mole in the light of the warm April sun, he emerged from the Cathedral and walked south along Amsterdam Avenue in the general direction of the American Museum of Natural History. During the long service, attended by only a fraction of the numbers Dean Pike had drawn thirty years earlier, he had unaccountably felt the need to touch base: with the museum in which his grandfather's mineral collection was displayed and studied, with the streets of the west Seventies and Eighties where he had lived as a student at Columbia, with the neighborhood's present mixture of ethnic groups and urban rehabbers. Probably the walk was longer than his doctor would have approved just yet. But it was a good day for sauntering, and he could stop for a rest and something to eat at one of the new restaurants behind the museum.

What a difference a few blocks or a few years makes in this city, he thought. In his student days, the Hispanics had only recently moved into this part of the West Side, and the Lincoln Center, with its complement of gay students and performing artists, was yet to come. He had been interested in both Mediterranean and Caribbean peoples from the days he was allowed to move the pins representing ship movements on the big map in his grandfather's office. Right after the war his grandparents had taken him to Havana, and he had felt a strange, almost chemical attraction to these tawny, doe-eyed boys of his own age who radiated a warmth he himself seemed to lack. A vacation in Italy with his great-aunt following prep school and an archaeological dig in the Cyclades the summer after his junior year in college had given him a deeper awareness of the culture of the Greeks and Italians in whose Manhattan neighborhoods he had always felt at home.

The middle fifties had been a season of hope for American cities. Many of his more idealistic contemporaries had committed themselves to living in the city and finding ways in which old and new could live together. In this spirit he had volunteered for a time in the Lower East Side Mission of Trinity Parish. He didn't really feel suited to the clergy, social work or planning, however, and much less to teaching or to following the business commitments of most of his male contemporaries. But he was moved by the great need of New York's newest immigrants for places where they could learn how to survive, not as needy "clients" or objects of benevolence, but as independent human beings working out their own life patterns.

In the end he shifted to the School of Library Service, added some intensive private courses in conversational Spanish, and emerged with both an M. A. in humanities and a master's degree in librarianship. After a year in the lower echelons of the New York Public Library system's bureaucracy, he applied for and was given a job nobody else wanted, the care of a new bi-lingual, store-front branch on this very Amsterdam Avenue. Still in the family groove, he thought wryly; for years his grandmother had done volunteer work on the same street, in the heavily dormered and gabled structure he was now passing, once the Home for Respectable Indigent Females.

For a couple of years things had gone very well. His little storefront library began to be something of a drop-in center for the neighborhood's elderly. He had started a "Reading is Fun" program for the younger kids, organized a preparatory course for the high school drop-outs and others looking toward a high school equivalency diploma, and even set up a bottomless coffee pot for the alkies, eccentrics and drifters who wandered in to get out of the cold or the rain.

As more and more Cubans fleeing the Castro regime entered the neighborhood, he developed a new kind of "Americanization" class which emphasized the cultural contributions the new immigrants were making to the city as well as what they needed to survive as new citizens. Many of these functions went beyond what the library system's bureaucrats had in mind, however. He had been warned more than once that his duties were to charge out books, collect and account for fines, maintain the flow of library statistical reports, and interpret the library's rules to "patrons," among whom should ideally not be alkies, eccentrics, drifters, non-reading elderly, and street corner toughs.

Throughout those years he had met other homosexuals through his contacts in the arts, in the library system, and in Village hot spots. He had even occasionally gone to poetry readings in the then very hip East Village, and it was there that he first heard Allen Ginsberg; it had been, he recalled, like meeting Whitman face to face. Through all this he had rigidly separated his personal and his professional life, and his sexual activity had been pretty discreetly managed. But one slow night, as he was locking up, one of the Cuban boys he had lured from a street gang and coached for the College Board exams burst in with the news that he had been accepted for early admission to Columbia on a full scholarship.

The day had brought another burst of nagging and recrimination from his library superiors, and the weather was as dismal and as bitter as only Manhattan in January can be. He was feeling very much alone, and probably looked it, when the radiantly happy youth reached out his arms to hug him in love and gratitude. One thing led to another, and the night guard found them together on the couch in the back room as he came by to check the security of the building. Within a week there was a hearing at which he was confronted both by the guard and by his library supervisor, told that his application for permanent employment by the city of New York would be denied, and advised that his immediate resignation would be in his own best interests as well as those of the New York Public Library system.

· · · · ·

The memory came back at him like a knife in the chest. He rested for a moment, and changed his direction toward the less threatening precincts of Central Park West. He had fled the city then; except for his cousins, there were no near ties. His share of the income of a family trust, and legacies from his grandmother and Aunt Susan, had sustained him until he had found a librarian's slot in a Boston-area research institution. For the next several years he carried an immense burden of interior guilt and shame, denied himself any outward sexual expression, and even cut himself off from his gay acquaintances in New York. No longer trusting the strength of his internal controls, he had kept a measured distance from all human interactions outside of the most formal situations: being a useful "extra man" at the occasional dinner party, attending concerts of the Boston Symphony, and the like.

Afraid now of the possible consequences of intimacy, he worked to extend his professional competence. He read widely, now and again wrote an elegantly worded essay read by a handful of his fellow professionals, and monitored the small signs of time eroding his features and dessicating his temperament. He watched everything from the sidelines, including himself. Christopher Isherwood had been right, he concluded, in lifting up the image of a camera for the ways in which homosexuals looked on themselves and the life of the world around them. By the time he was forty, he sensed that he was walking around in a many-layered, impermeable shell.

Then, in 1970, had come the opportunity to return to New York. It was a peculiar appointment. A friend of his grandfather named Lenox, something of a recluse in his later years, had been particularly affectionate toward the boy as he was growing up, and a source of moral support in the aftermath of his dismissal from the library system. Like an earlier member of his family in the nineteenth century, the old man had been a collector of books, manuscripts and art works. On his death in the early 1960's he had left some artistically distinguished family portraits to the New York Historical Society and a small collection of literary manuscripts to the Research Library at Fifth Avenue and 42nd Street.

Except for a caretaker's apartment in the basement, the old man's home near Gramercy Park had been shuttered for nearly a decade. People wondered why the house had never been sold, but assumed this was owing to the eccentricities of old Lenox's sister in California, the only surviving family member. Late in 1968, however, the sister too had passed away, and it was disclosed that she had only a life interest in the Lenox estate. The house itself, according to the obituary in the *New York Times*, was to be opened after her death as a specialized library and museum, heavily endowed and similar to the one established years earlier by J. P. Morgan less than twenty blocks away.

Early in 1970, after the estate had cleared probate, he had been asked by the Lenox executors to come to New York for a conference. There it was broken to him, in strictest confidence, that the focus of the proposed museum and library would be a collection of rare and unique materials documenting the creative experience of homosexuals and their impact on the Western cultural tradition. The will had specified that he was to be its first curator and director, should he wish. In a sealed letter addressed to him, Lenox had revealed his own life-long homosexuality, his growing suspicion that the grandson of his friend might be gay, and its confirmation by a private detective after the dismissal from the library system. Lenox's letter closed by urging him to take on these new responsibilities. Here, at least, he would be financially and administratively secure, and therefore free to experiment without fear of politicians on the make, city bureaucrats, and Federal witch-hunters.

After some intensive soul-searching, he had said yes. He took up residence in the modernized former servants' quarters on the top floor of the mansion and began to survey the collections. The old man had changed the major furnishings very little from the days of his own boyhood. A few early nineteenth century family heirlooms mingled incongruously with the heavy, dark furniture and panelling of an 1880's remodelling. But on the walls and tables and mantels were classic representations of gay art, most of it original, though there were a few nineteenth century copies of originals in European museums.

Among the art treasures were several depictions of Ganymede in painting and sculpture, from classical times to that of the Romantics. There was a small collection of Roman coins and other objects depicting the Emperor Hadrian and his beloved, Antinous. There was a magnificent grave stele showing a Greek ephebe of the time of Alexander the Great, several photographs of Sicilian youth inscribed to the collector by Baron von Gloeden himself, and not less than four of Henry Scott Tuke's sunlit paintings of willowy English fisher-lads bathing or playing naked on the Cornish shore. A separately alarmed heavy glass case contained an Attic black-figured vase dating from the 6th century B. C., showing a man's courtship of a youth and the latter's visible response, similar to the one in the collections of the Museum of Fine Arts in Boston, where it was only rarely displayed.

For three years, until the formal opening of the museum and library in 1973, the art works scattered among bank vaults, locked cabinets and closets had to be identified, the books catalogued, the manuscripts arranged, and climate-controlled research and storage spaces constructed. The sheer amount of preparatory work to be done, the research and concentration it demanded, and his own increasing commitment to the task, all acted as a kind of gentle therapy for a bruised identity.

It seemed that the collector had bought copies of almost every fine gay imprint from the invention of movable type, as well as a few manuscript works, including a corrupt Byzantine text of the Greek Anthology. There were complete runs of such privately printed imprints as the Cayme and Fortune presses, including one of the six copies of *Strato's Boyish Muse* containing etchings signed by the illustrator. A copy of Edward Perry Warren's pseudonyomous *Defence of Uranian Love*, by "Arthur Lyon Raile," was inscribed affectionately by the author. A set of corrected galleys from the first Kinsey Report and an advance copy of Donald Webster Cory's *The Homosexual in America* were among the items to be accessioned, as well as a scattering of gay apologias in the small press imprints of the middle and late 1950's, still in their original dust jackets.

But it was only after he turned to the correspondence files that he learned how extensively his grandfather's friend had been involved in gay creative expression. Some of the material had clearly been purchased: the manuscript of a Michelangelo sonnet, marked with his nephew's gender transpositions; some letters from Civil War troopers to Walt Whitman and two of his replies, and so forth. But far more interesting to him were personal notes from the aging Oscar Wilde, who had admired the youthful Lenox in fin de siècle Paris; letters from E. P. Warren and his circle at Lewes House, Sussex; and an extensive run of correspondence with Gertrude Stein and Virgil Thomson concerning the first production of *Four Saints in Three Acts*, which Mr. Lenox had helped finance. He found letters from Wilhelm von Gloeden, who had photographed the collector as a youth (fully clothed) at Taormina in 1887; from Amy Lowell, E. M. Forster, Natalie Barney and two or three others of her circle, and dozens more.

There were letters in French from an Austrian archduke who could not be immediately identified but with whom there had evidently been a whirlwind romance in Franz Josef's Vienna. There were letters in German from Magnus Hirschfeld, some soliciting research money and publication funds for his Institute for Sexual Science, and one describing the burning of the Institute and its priceless library at the hands of the Nazis in May, 1933. There was even correspondence from Thomas Mann documenting the collector's role as one of the models for Tadzio in "Death in Venice." Letters from Hart Crane often contained trial versions of poems for criticism. And at the bottom of a beautifully crafted steamer trunk he found not only correspondence with George Platt Lynes, chief fashion photographer for Vogue in 1930's, but nearly a hundred of Lynes' art deco photographs of male nudes, the negatives of which had been destroyed by the family after Lynes' death. In those years of preparation he had grieved over how much else of the documentation for gay contributions to Western and American civilization had been destroyed equally wantonly, lacking a place which might preserve it and make its rich content known.

He had not spent all his time shaping his new environment, however. As he worked toward the opening of the museum and library, scheduled for the donor's centenary in late September, 1973, he had become aware of what people were learning to call the "gay liberation" movement, its politics and its color, its supportive institutions and its openness about being "gay," not "queer" or "homosexual." Back in his Columbia days he had talked with a couple of members of the New York Mattachine Society at a party, and at their urging had attended a meeting or two. And he'd seen the odd issue of *One* and the *Mattachine Review*, picked up hastily at one of the New York newsstands carrying them. But at that point he just wasn't very comfortable with the idea of committing himself to a gay organization, or for that matter to any organization.

He had not been conspicuously more enamored of the politics of the new gay liberation groups as he saw them in the early 1970's. He was especially repelled by the frequent factionalism and by tawdry attempts to screen out the politically incorrect, including by ascription the white middle and upper class professional, of which he was clearly and indelibly one. As a political movement gay liberation engaged in too much wheel-spinning to be very effective, he thought, victimizing itself and its adherents with side issues and personal agendas which really didn't speak to the lives of most gays he knew anything about. On the other hand (and he was always to be ambivalent about it; hence "Yes, but" and "On the other hand"), increasingly one could bypass the more bizarre aspects of the movement and find something to do which was useful in direct human terms. And he had been much warmed by the efforts of often inexperienced and ill-informed, but extraordinarily open-hearted, gays of both genders struggling to create gay space, mutual aid groups, and other resources. They, at least, were reaching out with a helping hand in a still too troubled and troubling world.

In his interactions with a newer, freer gay generation he had often shared the feeling of Don Fabrizio in Giuseppe di Lampedusa's *The Leopard*, a novel he had read on its American publication in 1960 and thought both underrated by the critical establishment and too soon forgotten. "I belong to an unfortunate generation," said Fabrizio, "swung between the old world and the new, and I find myself ill at ease in both." Yet in practice he could, often enough, set aside his mental reservations, seeing his median position as that of a translator trying to wring meaning out of the old for the understanding of the new, pointing out some of the connections that needed to be made. Indeed, this was how he came to see his role as curator of the Lenox collection, though he sensed that at least some of the new free gays found him mildly archaic in his insistence on linking into and sustaining the older gay-influenced cultural and urban tradition.

He had begun to be sexually active again in the seventies. At first he discreetly employed a gay escort service which provided alert, college-trained models whom he could take to a special exhibition at the Metropolitan or to the revival of a medieval mystery play without embarassment before returning to his apartment for the night. These young gay men, and others he met in the course of his work in the museum and library, began in turn leading him to exhibits of contemporary gay art and performances in New York's emergent gay theatre. In 1974 he had even participated in the annual Christopher Street Gay Liberation Day parade, though he had abandoned the subsequent rally in distaste over its tendentious, divisive political rhetoric.

Almost without realizing it, and certainly without plan, he found himself becoming a mentor, a kind of reference point, a supportive if skeptical father-surrogate and occasional bed-mate for a fair number of questioning young men of a variety of styles and backgrounds, who were both discovering themselves and extending gay culture in the new atmosphere of freedom and creative self-expression. These encounters were often a learning experience for both parties. Though he reflexively maintained more than a touch of the old reserve, through these mentoring experiences he had an almost physical sense that at least some of the layers of shell around him were beginning to dissolve.

Gay liberation would never mean the same things for him as for these youngsters, to whom it was central in the formation of their identities. For him, its warmth percolated only gradually, melting the jagged edges of his sundered consciousness, and providing a healing cement for the divisions within. But also for him there would always be a residue of vulnerability, an edge of sadness, a wistful regret that his life had been fragmented so early, that so much of his energies had been spent badly, struggling to survive and become a whole person in a homophobic society. There was no changing that, he knew. Like the advantages he had enjoyed in coming of age in the New York of the fifties, this too had been a structured condition of his day and generation.

· · · · ·

The walk seemed longer than he had remembered it, and he felt himslf tiring. Resting for a while on a parapet overlooking Central Park, he could see the Metropolitan in the distance, through the trees. His mind turned again to the matter of continuities and relationships. In college he had read Robert M. Hutchins' *The Higher Learning in America*, and though in some ways the argument and the language seemed dated now, several phrases had stayed with him. One of them was this: "The aim of education is to connect man with man, to connect the present with the past, and to advance the thinking of the race."

About seven years before, as the date of the opening of the Lenox collection approached, he had begun to see the institution in these larger educational terms. He wanted to make it not simply a quarrying-ground for scholars, but a place where gays and their friends could both discover and advance a heritage which would be a legitimate source of gay pride. The opening was not reported by *The New York Times*, though the *Village Voice* and several gay papers had sent representatives. As the word spread, gays from the city and elsewhere began to come, singly or in pairs, though the standard general guides to New York City's cultural attractions still found reasons to omit it.

After a couple of years he had persuaded his board that the stables could be converted into a small conference center, with a browser's collection of lesbian and gay literature. In the former coachman's apartment above there would be room for the offices of gay cultural and arts organizations. Two of the trustees, one a noted civil rights lawyer and the other one of New York's first female senior bank executives, neither of them gay, had found the funding for it. After the insurance companies had forced the construction of a new fire wall between the stables and mansion and the hiring of around-the-clock security guards (drawn, as it developed, from the macho Lavender Panthers), the center had opened in September, 1976 with an exhibition and conference on "Lesbian and Gay Images in Art." Advance notices of the exhibition and even an offer of paid advertising were refused by the *Times*.

Nevertheless, the two facilities were now in place, one housing the tradition of gay culture and the other its cutting edge. But the real problem was to get young gay people to link the two, to see themselves in organic relationship with the urban culture of the past and with others, mostly non-gay, perhaps in the future mostly non-white, who still had the power to shape the future of the city. He was almost the last member of one of those old New York families committed to building up and supporting the cultural resources, structures and institutions without which New York would be simply a vast money and real estate machine. He knew that their day, and his, was past. But how to recreate this ethical tradition of urban and urbane commitment, and extend it to previously excluded groups?

He looked out over the restful panorama below him, smiling at the meeting of old and new within the range of his vision. That section of Central Park West had been a gay cruising-ground in his student days, and the stretch of heavy vegetation yonder had enclosed, he was told (he'd never explored it), a safe place for al fresco sex. Now, of course, a younger generation was observing exactly the same rituals in the same location, carrying on a tradition probably as old as Central Park itself.

Yet the safety of the park, as of the city, had declined enormously in the seventies, and there had been some brutal beatings of gay men within the park boundaries in the last year or so. Just in the last few weeks he had read of a frightening series of attacks on known or suspected lesbians or gay men on the nearby streets, and a leading gay activist had been run down by an automobile only about ten days earlier. Police reported "no leads" or "no suspects." But rumors surfacing in the gay community had reached him, to the effect that the persons responsible were a small group of Irish-American teenagers who had become enamored of tactics of the Irish Republican Army. It was even alleged that their leader was the son of a high New York police official previously suspected of diverting Law Enforcement Assistance Administration funds and weapons to the I.R.A., through nothing had been proven.

He had begun to walk again, along Central Park West. Turning to cross the street, he saw a Hispanic youth in his early twenties crossing diagonally ahead of him. The youth was wearing a brilliant tropical shirt, open to the navel, and form-fitting, slightly faded jeans. A tasteful but clearly visible jewelled earring was attached to his right earlobe and, to make matters even clearer, a shocking-pink lambda symbol was sewn onto his right rear pants pocket, over the edge of which peeped a dark blue handkerchief. Even straights are wearing left-ear earrings nowadays, thought the curator, which was still immensely confusing to one who had learned with difficulty the standard gay codes. But even in 1980, to see a male signal so boldly that he was unquivocally gay could still take him by surprise.

As the curator stepped between the crossing lines, a white Cadillac with a crumpled fender pulled to a halt just ahead of him. Two youths in kelly green tee-shirts jumped out and went after the Hispanic, yelling "faggot" as they ran. Almost before he had seen them, they were punching and kicking the young gay man, panicking elderly passersby out for a Sunday walk. Shaken out of his musings, the curator reverted to the reflexes of his basic training days and raced across Central Park West heedless of taxis, pedestrians and his own physical limitations. Trying to pull one of the attackers away, he was promptly sucker-punched by a third who slammed him against a nearby building and knocked off his glasses. Before he could pick himself up, he heard the three assailants running back to the car shouting "kill the fuckin' queers," felt a tightening in his chest, and blacked out.

• • • •

As he recovered consciousness, he felt himself struggling against an oxygen nose cone and sensed rather than felt the body of a young EMT who was bending over him just far enough to expose a Lambda pendant suspended from a neck chain. Then he became aware of a small knot of habitually curious New Yorkers gathered around to gawk, as well as the flashing lights of an ambulance into which two other EMT's were putting a loaded stretcher. "Is the boy all right?" he asked, realizing as soon as he said it that, given all circumstances, it was a pretty stupid question.

"He'll pull through, in spite of what those bastards tried to do to him," replied the EMT. "But you gave us a real scare. Good thing you had that heart I.D. bracelet on you. We're running him up to St. Luke's for x-rays on his rib cage, and we'd like to have one of the doctors there check you over for any sign of concussion, if you don't mind, sir. The cops'll talk to you at the hospital."

He was going to refuse, but the size of the bandage on his head made him think he probably resembled the Duchess in Tenniel's illustrations for *Alice in Wonderland*. Inside the ambulance the other man lay quietly, his colorful shirt shredded and his smooth amber torso covered with bruises and bandages. The curator leaned over the youth and spoke a few words of comfort in halting Spanish. He was rewarded with a hesitant smile and then a playfully questioning glance from the most appealing black eyes he had seen for as long as he could remember.

Then he realized that the EMT was talking to him again. "Have I met you before?" he asked, vaguely remembering the face but not the context. The EMT replied that he and his lover had visited the museum and library a couple of months back. After the curator learned that they had read Whitman in high school, he had shown them the unbowdlerized manuscript copy of the 1860 edition of *Leaves of Grass*. "You told us how Whitman had to change the pronouns from male to female," said the EMT, "which is what Jack and I have to do too, sometimes. So we started reading up on Whitman and last weekend we went out on the Long Island to South Huntington, to see his birthplace. Y'know, that collection of yours has really done a lot for us. Some of our friends think that gays didn't exist before disco. But the stuff you shared with us really puts us in touch with ourselves."

In the emergency waiting room the EMT gave each of them a parting hug, somewhat to the disapproval of the nurse at the screening station. The younger man was a little frightened by the bustle and the impersonality of it all. After the police left, they found a quiet corner and talked softly in Spanish while they waited for the x-ray technicians. His own Spanish was rusty, but it seemed more appropriate for him to enter the youth's culture, and in any case what was passing between them didn't depend entirely on verbal forms.

By the time he had seen the doctor and left the hospital, where the younger man was detained overnight, he had learned that his new friend has escaped from a Cuban prison three years before, had just finished at the city's Hostos Community College, but had not yet found the regular job he needed to support himself through further years of schooling. Currently he was washing dishes weekends in a gay restaurant in exchange for his meals, and living in a basement room next to the furnace in return for taking out the trash. This had left him with time to be active in a new Hispanic gay rights group and to work behind the scenes in the productions of a new gay theatre, where he'd seen the curator a couple of times in the audience. Somehow also a message was conveyed that he liked to be with older men, especially middle-aged Don Quixotes who lacked the practical wisdom needed to realize that they had no business trying singlehandedly to rescue young gay activists from roving gangs of youthful queer-bashers.

It was for good reason, the curator told himself in the taxicab, that the Greeks had held the relationship of lovers to be both a sacred and a civic responsibility. Who knew what lay ahead for him and for this latest of gay immigrants, should they decide to spend their futures in the care of each other and in the creation of a new gay world? The bonds which tied them were not recognised in law, but neither were those other bonds which would be necessary to heal the divided city and to enhance its life: the bonds of civility, of integrity, of loving concern, of mutuality, which were the ultimate way out of the cycle of urban decay. Their bonding might stand for a symbol of that larger promise which the city held for all of its residents, and especially for its gay citizens, if these elusive kinds of connections could be realized in their own lifetimes.

Back home in his study, he pulled out his well-worn copy of Sir Richard Livingstone's *Pageant of Greece* and turned, as he often did, to the speech of Pericles at the Anthesteria. "We are lovers of beauty without extravagance," he read, "and lovers of wisdom without unmanliness. Wealth to us is not mere means for display but an opportunity for achievement; and poverty we think it no disgrace to acknowledge, but a real degradation to make no effort to overcome. Our citizens attend to both public and private duties, and do not allow absorption in their own various affairs to interfere with their knowledge of the city's." Indeed, he thought, "the busy spectacle of our great city's life as we have it before us day by day" compelled a response of obligation and commitment to the meeting of self-evident needs. Was this a contemporary form that the gay contribution to the cultural life of his own metropolis might usefully take?

Pleased with the thought, and anticipating a visit to St. Luke's in the morning, he checked the daily report of the museum guard, fed the cat and himself, found his pen and a large yellow pad, and began to write more intensely than he had ever dared write before.

· · · · ·

(from The New York Times, Tuesday, April 29, 1980)

Museum Curator, 49, Dies

The body of Richard Gardiner Blydenburgh, Curator of the Lenox Museum and Library on East Nineteenth Street, was found at his writing-desk early yesterday morning by a museum guard. Mr. Blydenburgh, who would have been fifty years old on May 16th, had recently been undergoing treatment for a heart condition.

He was born in St. George, Staten Island, the only child of the late Addison T. and Eleanor Gardiner (Greene) Blydenburgh, and christened at St. John's Episcopal Church. On his father's side he was a descendant of Governor Peter Stuyvesant; on his mother's, of Lion Gardiner, first Proprietor of Gardiner's Island. His great-aunt, the late Susan Scofield Greene, was for many years Director of the New York Humane Society.

Mr. Blydenburgh was graduated with highest honors from Swarthmore College in 1952, following which he served with the United States Army in Japan. After two years of graduate study at Columbia University, he worked as a librarian in the New York Public Library system and as Curator of Rare Books and Manuscripts in the Museum of Comparative Zoology in Cambridge, Mass. He had been Curator of the Lenox collection since 1970.

The afternoon before his death Mr. Blydenburgh had been involved in an apparent attempt to prevent the beating of a Cuban-born youth by a group of assailants near the American Museum of Natural History, of which his grandfather, the late Francis Stewart Greene, a customs broker and amateur mineralogist, had been a trustee. Leaders of the city's homosexual community have claimed that this attack, following a number of such incidents in recent months, demonstrates that the municipal government is incompetent to provide protection for open or apparent homosexual persons in New York City. Alleging that those responsible for these attacks are the sons of highly placed city officials, they have called for a Federal grand jury investigation of alleged conspiracy to violate the civil rights of Mr. Blydenburgh, of the young man who was the primary target of the assault, and of other "gay activists" in the city of New York.

The city coroner, in a report issued through police department headquarters, has officially ruled the cause of death to be "heart failure," citing Mr. Blydenburgh's recent medical history. Police and city officials have denied allegations made against the named youths, who have not been taken into custody. One high city official, who refused to be identified, is quoted as saying that the youths accused of the assult may well have been morally offended by witnessing what, he asserted, was a blatant attempt to solicit "a Spic who was obviously hanging around waiting for a john." The official commented further that "we need more vigilant youth like these to assist the endeavors of the police to keep perverts off the public streets."

A Liturgy of the Resurrection will be sung on Thursday at 11 A. M. in the Cathedral of St. John the Divine. The Rt. Rev. Paul Moore, Jr., Bishop of New York, will deliver the eulogy. Following the service, the body is to be cremated; the ashes will be placed in the Cathedral crypt at the convenience of the family.

A memorial service sponsored by Integrity/New York, a Greenwich Village homosexual organization, will be held at 2 P.M. Sunday at the Church of St. Luke in the Fields, 485 Hudson Street. A group calling itself the "Gay Activist's Alliance" has announced that it will sponsor a march from Washington Square to City Hall on Monday evening, to be followed by a demonstration and rally at City Hall Park at which the other alleged beating victim, Carlos Santamaria, will speak. Police officials say the group's request for a permit has been denied, and that any attempt to hold an illegal protest would be met with an appropriate level of force.

Mr. Blydenburgh is survived by a cousin, Theodore VanWyck Blydenburgh, M.D., Chief of Surgery at Roosevelt Hospital and a well-known social and civic figure. Yesterday afternoon Dr. Blydenburgh appeared with several homosexual activists at a hastily called press conference and announced that, in accordance with the deceased's express wishes, the income from a family trust will provide for a community scholarship fund "in support of the post-secondary education of New York's lesbian and gay youth of all races and creeds."